LAND ROVER
3.5, 3.9, 4.0, 4.2 & 4.6
V8 PETROL ENGINES
OVERHAUL MANUALS

These engines, with or without Suffix B
added to the engine serial number are
fitted to the following models:

Discovery
Defender
Range Rover Classic

Publication Part No. LRL 0164ENG
Published by Land Rover Limited
© 1997 Copyright Land Rover Limited

INTRODUCTION

How to use this Manual

To assist in the use of this Manual the section title is given at the top and the relevant sub-section is given at the bottom of each page.

This manual contains procedures for overhaul of the V8 engine on the bench with the gearbox, clutch, inlet manifold, exhaust manifolds, coolant pump, starter motor, alternator, and all other ancillary equipment removed. For information regarding General Information, Adjustments, removal of oil seals, engine units and ancillary equipment, consult the Repair Manual.

This manual is divided into 3 sections:
- Data, Torque & Tools
- Description and Operation and
- Overhaul

To assist filing of revised information each sub-section is numbered from page 1.

Individual items are to be overhauled in the sequence in which they appear in this manual. Items numbers in the illustrations are referred to in the text.

Overhaul operations include reference to Service tool numbers and the associated illustration depicts the tool. Where usage is not obvious the tool is shown in use. Land Rover tool numbers are quoted, for the equivalent Rover Cars tool number refer to the Service Tool section. Operations also include reference to wear limits, relevant data, and specialist information and useful assembly details.

WARNINGS, CAUTIONS and **NOTES** have the following meanings:

 WARNING: Procedures which must be followed precisely to avoid the possibility of injury.

 CAUTION: Calls attention to procedures which must be followed to avoid damage to components.

 NOTE: Gives helpful information.

Engine serial number

The engine serial number and conpression ratio will be found stamped on a cast pad on the cylinder block between numbers 3 and 5 cylinders. The compression ratio is above the serial number.

References

With the engine and gearbox assembly removed, the crankshaft pulley end of the engine is referred to as the front. References to RH and LH banks of cylinders are taken viewing from the flywheel end of the engine.

Operations covered in this Manual do not include reference to testing the vehicle after repair. It is essential that work is inspected and tested after completion and if necessary a road test of the vehicle is carried out particularly where safety related items are concerned.

Dimensions

The dimensions quoted are to design engineering specification with Service Limits where applicable.

REPAIRS AND REPLACEMENTS

When replacement parts are required it is essential that only Land Rover recommended parts are used.

Attention is particularly drawn to the following points concerning repairs and the fitting of replacement parts and accessories.

Torque wrench setting figures given in this Manual must be used. Locking devices, where specified, must be fitted. If the efficiency of a locking device is impaired during removal it must be renewed.

The terms of the vehicle warranty may be invalidated by the fitting of parts other than Land Rover recommended parts. All Land Rover recommended parts have the full backing of the vehicle warranty.

Land Rover dealers are obliged to supply only Land Rover recommended parts.

SPECIFICATION

Land Rover are constantly seeking to improve the specification, design and production of their vehicles and alterations take place accordingly. While every effort has been made to ensure the accuracy of this Manual, it should not be regarded as an infallible guide to current specifications of any particular vehicle.

This Manual does not constitute an offer for sale of any particular component or vehicle. Land Rover dealers are not agents of the Company and have no authority to bind the manufacturer by any expressed or implied undertaking or representation.

DATA

Firing order	1, 8, 4, 3, 6, 5, 7, 2	
	Cylinders 1, 3, 5, 7 - LH side of engine	
	Cylinders 2, 4, 6, 8 - RH side of engine	

Cylinder head

Maximum warp	0.05 mm	0.002 in
Reface limit from new	0.50 mm	0.02 in

Valve springs

Free length	48.30 mm	1.90 in
Fitted length	40.40 mm	1.60 in
Load at fitted length	339 ± 10 N	76 ± 2 lbf
Load at valve open length	736 ± 10 N	165 ± 2 lbf

Valves

Valve stem diameter:		
Inlet	8.664 to 8.679 mm	0.341 to 0.342 in
Exhaust	8.651 to 8.666 mm	0.340 to 0.341 in
Valve head diameter:		
Inlet	39.75 to 40.00 mm	1.5 to 1.6 in
Exhaust	34.226 to 34.480 mm	1.3 to 1.4 in
Valve installed height - maximum	47.63 mm	1.9 in
Valve stem to guide clearance:		
Inlet	0.025 to 0.066 mm	0.001 to 0.002 in
Exhaust	0.038 to 0.078 mm	0.0015 to 0.003 in

Valve guides

Valve guide installed height	15.0 mm	0.59 in
Inside diameter after reaming	8.7 mm	0.34 in

Valve seats

Valve seat width:		
Inlet	36.83 mm	1.45 in
Exhaust	31.50 mm	1.24 in
Valve seat angle	46° to 46° 25'	
Valve seating width:		
Inlet	0.89 to 1.4 mm	0.035 to 0.055 in
Exhaust	1.32 to 1.83 mm	0.052 to 0.072 in
Valve face angle	45°	

Oil pump - Engine numbers without suffix B

Gear to cover face minimum clearance	0.05 mm	0.002 in

Oil pressure relief valve - Engine numbers without suffix B

Spring free length	81.28 mm	3.2 in

INFORMATION

Oil pump - Engine numbers with suffix B

Inner to outer rotor clearance - maximum	0.25 mm	0.01 in
Rotors to cover plate clearance - maximum	0.1 mm	0.004 in
Drive gear wear step depth - maximum	0.15 mm	0.006 in

Oil pressure relief valve - Engine numbers with suffix B

Spring free length	60.0 mm	2.4 in

Camshaft

Maximum run-out	0.05 mm	0.002 in
End-float - Camshafts with thrust plate	0.05 to 0.35 mm	0.002 to 0.014 in

Piston rings

Ring to groove clearance:		
Top compression	0.05 to 0.10 mm	0.002 to 0.004 in
2nd compression	0.05 to 0.10 mm	0.002 to 0.004 in
Ring fitted gap:		
Top compression	0.44 to 0.57 mm	0.02 to 0.022 in
2nd compression	0.44 to 0.57 mm	0.02 to 0.022 in
Oil control rails	0.38 to 1.40 mm	0.014 to 0.05 in
Oil control ring width	3.00 mm	0.12 in - maximum

Pistons

Clearance in bore, measured at bottom of skirt at right angles to bore	0.02 to 0.045 mm	0.001 to 0.002 in

Gudgeon pins

Length	72.67 to 72.79 mm	2.85 to 2.86 in
Diameter	22.215 to 22.220 mm	0.87 to 0.871 in
Clearance in piston	0.006 to 0.015 mm	0.0002 to 0.0006 in

Connecting rods

Length between centres	143.71 to 143.81 mm	5.66 to 5.67 in

Cylinder bore

Cylinder bore diameter:		
3.5 engine	88.90 mm	3.5 in
3.9 engine	94.00 mm	3.7 in
4.2 engine	94.00 mm	3.7 in
Maximum ovality	0.013 mm	0.0005 in

Crankshaft

Main journal diameter	58.409 to 58.422 mm	2.29 to 2.30 in
Maximum regrind diameter	57.900 to 57.914 mm	2.28 to 2.281 in
Maximum out of round	0.040 mm	0.002 in
Big-end journal diameter	50.800 to 50.812 mm	1.99 to 2.00 in
Maximum regrind diameter	50.292 to 50.305 mm	1.97 to 1.98 in
Maximum out of round	0.040 mm	0.002 in
End-float	0.10 to 0.20 mm	0.004 to 0.008 in
Maximum run-out	0.08 mm	0.003 in
Spigot bearing inside diameter	19.177 + 0.025 - 0.00 mm	0.75 + 0.001 - 0.00 in

Main bearings

Main bearing diametrical clearance	0.010 to 0.048 mm	0.0004 to 0.002 in
Undersizes	0.254, 0.508 mm	0.01, 0.02 in

Big-end bearings

Big-end bearing diametrical clearance	0.015 to 0.055 mm	0.0006 to 0.0021 in
Undersizes	0.254, 0.508 mm	0.01, 0.02 in
Endfloat on journal	0.15 to 0.36 mm	0.006 to 0.01 in

Flywheel

Flywheel minimum thickness	39.93 mm	1.6 in

Drive plate

Drive plate setting height	8.08 to 8.20 mm	0.32 to 0.33 in

SERVICE TOOLS

Land Rover Number	Rover Number	Description
LRT-12-010*	18G 1014*	Protection sleeve - crankshaft rear oil seal
LRT-12-013	18G 1150	Remover/replacer gudgeon pin
LRT-12-014	18G 1150E	Adapter remover/replacer gudgeon pin
LRT-12-034	18G 1519	Valve spring compressor
LRT-12-037	RO.274401	Drift remover - valve guide
LRT-12-038	RO.600959	Drift replacer - valve guide
LRT-12-055		Distance piece - valve guide
LRT-12-089**		Replacer - timing cover oil seal
LRT-12-090**		Retainer - oil pump gears
LRT-12-091**		Replace - crankshaft rear oil seal
LRT-12-095**		Protection sleeve - crankshaft rear oil seal
LRT-12-501	MS76B	Basic handle set - valve seat cutters
LRT-12-503	MS150-8.5	Adjustable valve seat pilot
LRT-12-515	RO.605774A	Distance piece - valve guide
LRT-12-517	-	Adjustable valve seat cutter

* Engine numbers without
suffix B
** Engine numbers with
suffix B

Service tools must be obtained direct from the manufacturers:

V.L. Churchill,
P.O. Box No 3,
London Road,
Daventry,
Northants, NN11 4NF.
England.

ENGINE

Crankshaft pulley bolt	270 Nm	200 lbf.ft
Timing cover to cylinder block bolts	22 Nm	16 lbf.ft
Camshaft gear bolt	50 Nm	37 lbf.ft
Rocker cover bolts: +		
Stage 1	4 Nm	3 lbf.ft
Stage 2	8 Nm	6 lbf.ft
Stage 3 - Re-torque to	8 Nm	6 lbf.ft
Rocker shaft to cylinder head bolts	38 Nm	28 lbf.ft
Cylinder head bolts - Engine numbers without suffix B: + *		
Bolts 11 to 14 - Outer row	60 Nm	44 lbf.ft
Bolts 2, 4, 6, 8 and 10 - Centre row	90 Nm	66 lbf.ft
Bolts 1, 3, 5, 7 and 9 - Inner row	90 Nm	66 lbf.ft
Cylinder head bolts - Engine numbers with suffix B: + *		
Stage 1	20 Nm	15 lbf.ft
Stage 2	Then 90°	
Stage 3	Further 90°	
Lifting eye to cylinder head bolts	40 Nm	30 lbf.ft
Connecting rod nuts/bolts	50 Nm	37 lbf.ft
Main bearing cap bolts +**		
Initial torque - all bolts:	14 Nm	10 lbf.ft
Final torque:		
Numbers 1 to 4 main bearing cap bolts:	70 Nm	52 lbf.ft
Rear main bearing cap bolts:	90 Nm	66 lbf.ft
Flywheel bolts	80 Nm	59 lbf.ft
Drive plate assembly bolts	45 Nm	33 lbf.ft
Drive plate adapter Allen screws	85 Nm	63 lbf.ft
Oil sump drain plug	45 Nm	33 lbf.ft
Oil sump bolts +	23 Nm	17 lbf.ft
Oil pressure relief valve plug - Engine numbers without suffix B	45 Nm	33 lbf.ft
Oil pump cover to timing cover - Engine numbers without suffix B	12 Nm	9 lbf.ft
Oil pump cover plate screws - Engine numbers with suffix B ***	4 Nm	3 lbf.ft
Oil pump cover plate bolt - if fitted ***	8 Nm	6 lbf.ft
Oil pressure switch	15 Nm	11 lbf.ft
Oil strainer bolts	10 Nm	7 lbf.ft
Distributor clamp nut	20 Nm	15 lbf.ft
Spark plug	20 Nm	15 lbf.ft
Coolant pump/timing cover to cylinder block	22 Nm	16 lbf.ft
Camshaft thrust plate bolts - if fitted	25 Nm	18 lbf.ft

+   Tighten in sequence
*   Lightly oil threads prior to assembly.
**   Coat threads with lubricant EXP16A (Marston Lubricants) prior to assembly.
***   Coat threads with Loctite 222 prior to assembly.

INFORMATION

GENERAL

For bolts and nuts not otherwise specified:

METRIC

M5	4 Nm	3 lbf.ft
M6	6 Nm	4 lbf.ft
M8	18 Nm	13 lbf.ft
M10	35 Nm	26 lbf.ft
M12	65 Nm	48 lbf.ft
M14	80 Nm	59 lbf.ft
M16	130 Nm	96 lbf.ft

UNC / UNF

1/4	9 Nm	7 lbf.ft
5/16	25 Nm	18 lbf.ft
3/8	40 Nm	30 lbf.ft
7/16	75 Nm	55 lbf.ft
1/2	90 Nm	66 lbf.ft
5/8	135 Nm	100 lbf.ft

CONTENTS

Page

ENGINE

CONTENTS

This page is intentionally left blank

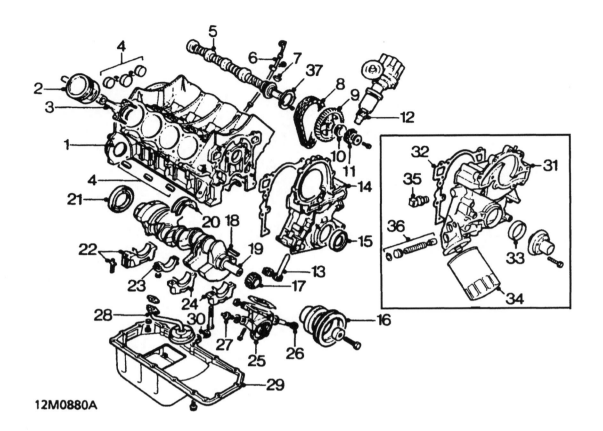

12M0880A

CYLINDER BLOCK COMPONENTS

1. Cylinder block
2. Piston and gudgeon pin
3. Connecting rod
4. Core plugs
5. Camshaft
6. Dipstick
7. Camshaft key
8. Timing chain
9. Camshaft sprocket
10. Spacer
11. Distributor drive gear - if fitted
12. Distributor - if fitted
13. Oil pump gears *
14. Timing cover and gasket *
15. Timing cover oil seal *
16. Crankshaft pulley
17. Crankshaft sprocket
18. Woodruff key
19. Crankshaft

20. Centre main bearing shell - upper
21. Crankshaft rear oil seal
22. Rear main bearing cap and side seals
23. Connecting rod cap
24. Main bearing caps
25. Oil pump cover *
26. Oil pressure relief valve assembly *
27. Oil pressure switch *
28. Oil pump suction pipe and strainer
29. Sump
30. Drain plug
31. Timing cover **
32. Timing cover gasket **
33. Timing cover oil seal **
34. Oil filter **
35. Oil pressure switch **
36. Oil pressure relief valve assembly **
37. Camshaft thrust plate - if fitted

* Engine numbers without suffix B
** Engine numbers with suffix B

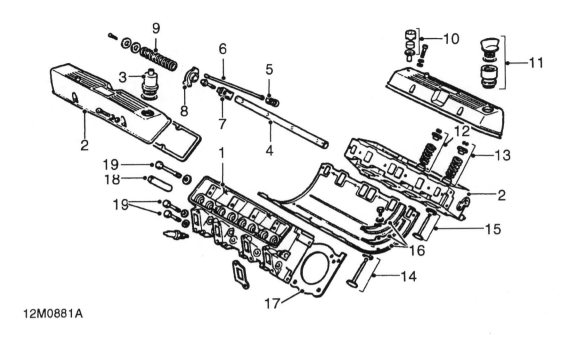

12M0881A

CYLINDER HEAD COMPONENTS

1. Cylinder head
2. Rocker cover
3. PCV filter
4. Rocker shaft
5. Tappet
6. Pushrod
7. Rocker shaft bracket
8. Rocker arm
9. Rocker shaft spring
10. PCV air intake filter

11. Engine oil filler cap
12. Inlet valve seal, spring, cap, and collets
13. Exhaust valve seal, spring, cap and collets
14. Inlet valve and seat
15. Exhaust valve and seat
16. Inlet manifold gasket and seals
17. Cylinder head gasket
18. Valve guide
19. Bolts - cylinder head

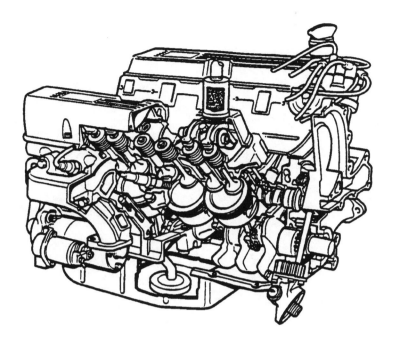

12M1087

Engine without suffix B added to serial no. illustrated

OPERATION

The V8 engine is an eight cylinder, water cooled unit comprising of cast aluminium cylinder block and cylinder heads.

The two banks of cast iron cylinder liners are shrink fitted and are located on stops in the cylinder block. The banks of cylinders are set at 90° to each other. The crankshaft is carried in five main bearings, end-float being controlled by the thrust faces of the upper centre main bearing shell.

The centrally located camshaft is driven by the crankshaft via an inverted tooth chain. The valves are operated by rockers, pushrods and hydraulic tappets. The distributor - if fitted, is driven by a skew gear from the front of the camshaft.

The aluminium alloy, pistons have two compression rings and an oil control ring and are secured to the connecting rods by semi-floating gudgeon pins. On later 4.2L engines the gudgeon pin is offset 0.5 mm (0.02 in), identified by an arrow mark on the piston crown, which must always point to the front of the engine. Plain, big-end bearing shells are fitted to each connecting rod.

Lubrication - Engine numbers without suffix B

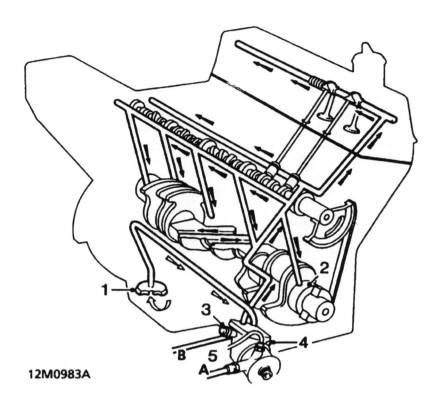

12M0983A

1. Oil strainer
2. Crankshaft main bearing oil feed
3. Oil pressure relief valve
4. Oil pump

5. Main gallery
   A Oil to cooler
   B Oil from cooler

Lubrication - Engine numbers with suffix B

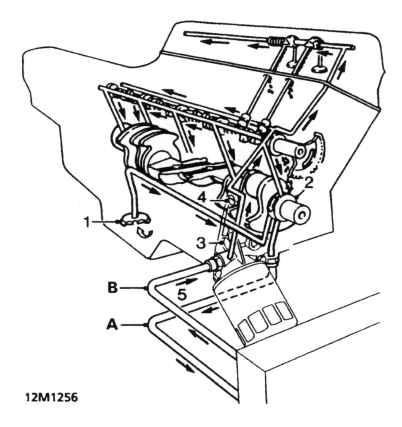

12M1256

1. Oil strainer
2. Oil pump
3. Pressure relief valve
4. Oil pressure switch

5. Main gallery
   A Oil to cooler
   B Oil from cooler

Engine numbers without suffix B

The full flow lubrication system uses an external gear pump which is driven by the distributor drive shaft. The oil pump gears are housed in the timing cover and the oil pressure relief valve and warning light switch are fitted to the oil pump cover.

Engine numbers with suffix B

The full flow lubrication system uses a gear type oil pump driven from the crankshaft. The assembly is integral with the timing cover which also carries the full flow oil filter, oil pressure switch and pressure relief valve.

All engines

Oil is drawn from the pressed steel sump through a strainer and into the oil pump, excess pressure being relieved by the pressure relief valve. The oil pressure warning light switch is screwed into the oil pump cover and registers the oil pressure in the main oil gallery on the outflow side of the filter. Pressurised oil passes through an oil cooler - if fitted to the full flow oil filter and through internal drillings to the crankshaft where it is directed to each main bearing and to the big end bearings via Nos. 1, 3 and 5 main bearings. An internal drilling in the cylinder block directs oil to the camshaft where it passes through further internal drillings to the hydraulic tappets, camshaft journals and rocker shaft. Lubrication to the thrust side of the cylinders is by oil grooves machined in each connecting rod big end joint face, which are timed to align with holes in the big end journals on the power and exhaust strokes.

Distributor drive and timing chain lubrication

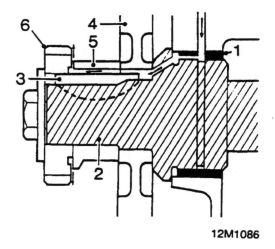

12M1086

Hydraulic tappets

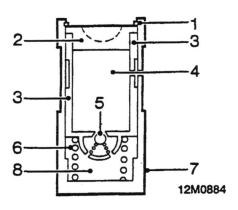

12M0884

1. Bearing
2. Camshaft
3. Key
4. Camshaft timing chain sprocket
5. Spacer
6. Distributor drive gear

The distributor drive and timing chain are lubricated from the camshaft front bearing. The feed to the timing chain is channelled along the camshaft sprocket, key and spacer.

1. Clip
2. Pushrod seat
3. Inner sleeve
4. Upper chamber
5. Non-return ball valve
6. Spring
7. Outer sleeve
8. Lower chamber - high pressure

The purpose of the hydraulic tappet is to provide maintenance free and quiet operation of the inlet and exhaust valves. It achieves this by utilising engine oil pressure to eliminate the mechanical clearance between the rockers and the valve stems.

During normal operation, engine oil pressure present in the upper chamber passes through the non-return ball valve and into the lower, high pressure, chamber.

When the cam begins to lift the outer sleeve, the resistance of the valve spring felt through the push rod and seat causes the tappet inner sleeve to move downwards inside the outer sleeve. This downward movement of the inner sleeve closes the ball valve and increases the pressure in the lower, high pressure chamber, sufficiently to ensure that the push rod opens the valve fully.

As the tappet moves off the peak of the cam the ball valve opens to equalise the pressure in both chambers which ensures the valve closes when the tappet is on the back of the cam.

ROCKER SHAFTS

Rocker shafts - remove

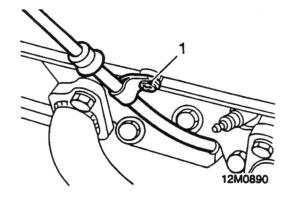

12M0890

1. *LH rocker shaft only:* Remove screw securing dipstick tube to rocker cover.

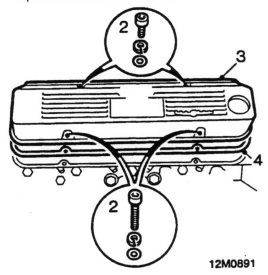

12M0891

2. Remove 4 Allen screws securing rocker cover to cylinder head.

⚠ NOTE: Note fitted position of 2 long screws. Later engines - multi-hex bolts are used.

3. Remove rocker cover.
4. Remove and discard gasket from rocker cover.
5. Mark each rocker shaft in relation to original cylinder head.

⚠ CAUTION: Incorrect fitment of rocker shafts will lead to an oil feed restriction.

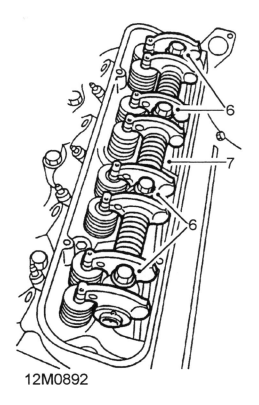

12M0892

6. Progressively slacken and remove 4 bolts securing rocker shaft assembly to cylinder head.
7. Remove rocker shaft assembly.
8. Remove pushrods and store in fitted order.
9. Repeat above procedures for remaining rocker shaft.

Rocker shafts - dismantling

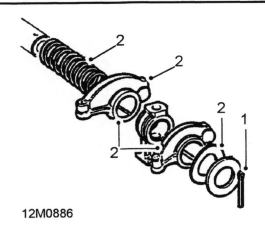

12M0886

1. Remove and discard split pin from one end of rocker shaft.
2. Remove plain washer, wave washer, rocker arms, brackets and springs.

Inspecting components

1. Thoroughly clean components.
2. Inspect each component for wear, in particular rocker arms and shafts. Discard weak or broken springs.
3. Inspect push rod seats in rocker arms.
4. Check push rods for straightness and inspect ball ends for damage, replace as necessary.

Rocker shafts - assembling

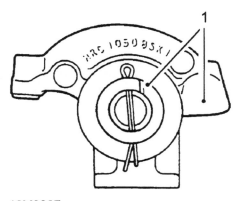

12M0887

1. Assemble rocker shafts with identification groove at one o'clock position with push rod end of rocker arm to the right.

 CAUTION: If rocker shafts are incorrectly assembled and fitted to engine, oil supply to rocker arms will be restricted.

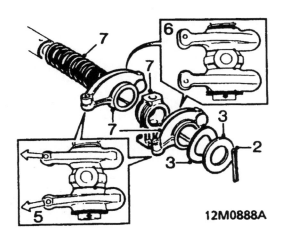

12M0888A

7. Assemble rocker arms, brackets and springs to rocker shaft.
8. Compress springs, fit wave washer, plain washer and secure with new split pin.

2. Fit new split pin to one end of rocker shaft.
3. Fit plain washer and wave washer.
4. Lubricate rocker arm bushes with clean engine oil.
5. Early type rocker arms are angled, and must be fitted with the valve end of the rocker arms angled away from each other as illustrated.
6. On later type rocker arms the valve end is offset and must be fitted as illustrated.

 NOTE: Early and late rocker arms are interchangeable provided the complete set is changed.

Rocker shafts - refit

1. Lubricate push rods with engine oil.
2. Fit push rods in removed order.

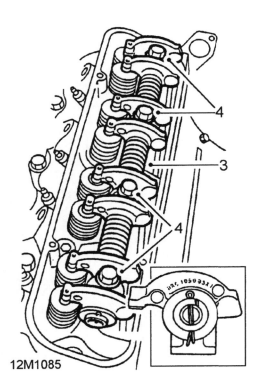

12M1085

3. Fit each rocker shaft assembly, ensuring identification groove is uppermost and towards front of engine on RH side and towards rear of engine on LH side.

 CAUTION: Incorrect fitment will result in an oil feed restriction.

4. Fit bolts and tighten to 38 Nm (28 lbf.ft).
5. Clean gasket surface in rocker cover using Bostik cleaner 6001 or equivalent, and allow to dry.

6. Apply a thin coating of Bostik 1775 or equivalent impact adhesive to mating surfaces of rocker cover and gasket.
7. Allow adhesive to cure, then fit gasket to rocker cover.

⚠ **CAUTION: Gasket fits one way round only, it must be fitted accurately as subsequent movement will destroy bonding. Allow cover to stand for 30 minutes before fitting.**

8. Fit rocker cover to cylinder head, fit Allen screws/multi-hex bolts and tighten by diagonal selection to:
    Stage 1 - 4 Nm (3 lbf.ft)
    Stage 2 - 8 Nm (6 lbf.ft)
    Stage 3 - Re-torque to 8 Nm (6 lbf.ft)

⚠ **CAUTION: The 2 short screws/bolts must be fitted on side of cover nearest centre of engine.**

9. **LH rocker shaft only:** Align dipstick tube to rocker cover, fit and tighten screw.

CYLINDER HEAD

Cylinder head - remove

1. Remove rocker shaft assembly.
2. Mark heads LH and RH for reassembly.

Engine numbers without suffix B

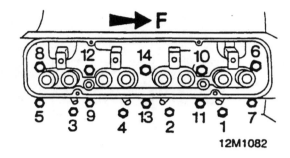

12M1082

 NOTE: RH cylinder head illustrated

3. Using sequence shown, remove 14 bolts securing cylinder head to cylinder block.

Engine numbers with suffix B

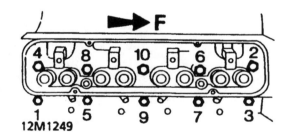

12M1249

 NOTE: RH cylinder head illustrated

4. Using sequence shown, remove and discard 10 bolts securing cylinder head to cylinder block.

NOTE: No bolts are fitted in the four lower holes in each cylinder head.

All engines

5. Release cylinder head from 2 dowels and remove cylinder head.
6. Remove and discard cylinder head gasket.

Valves and springs - remove

1. Remove spark plugs.

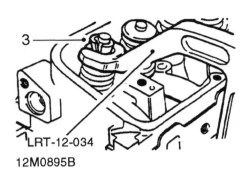

LRT-12-034

12M0895B

2. Using valve spring compressor **LRT-12-034** or a suitable alternative, compress valve spring.
3. Remove 2 collets.

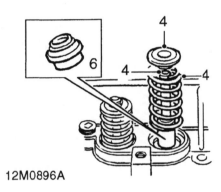

12M0896A

4. Release spring compressor and remove valve, valve spring cap and valve spring.
5. Repeat above operations for remaining valves.

 CAUTION: Keep valves, springs, caps and collets in fitted order.

6. Remove and discard valve stem oil seals.

Cylinder head - inspection

1. Clean all traces of gasket material from cylinder head using a plastic scraper.
2. Check core plugs for signs of leakage and corrosion, replace as necessary. Apply Loctite 572 to threads of screwed core plugs.

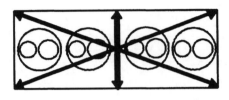

12M2902A

3. Check gasket face of each cylinder head for warping, across centre and from corner to corner:
   Maximum warp = 0.05 mm (0.002 in)

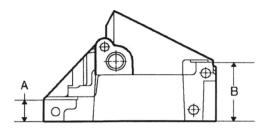

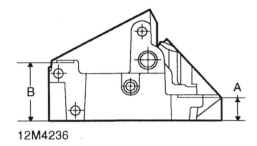

12M4236

Valves, valve springs and guides - inspection

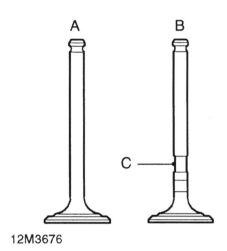

12M3676

4. Check cylinder head height at each end of cylinder head:

Engine numbers without suffix B
A= 23.9 mm (0.94 in) - new
B= 63.5 mm (2.5 in) - new

Engine numbers with suffix B
A= 22.94 mm (0.903 in) - new
B= 62.56 mm (2.463 in) - new

5. Cylinder heads may be refaced:
Reface limit = 0.50 mm (0.02 in) from new dimension.

△ NOTE: Two types of exhaust valve may be fitted - standard valves A in illustration or carbon break valves - B in illustration. Carbon break valves may be identified by the machined profile C on the valve stem. To prevent exhaust valves sticking, standard exhaust valves should be replaced with carbon break valves during engine overhaul.

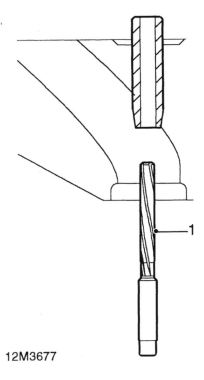

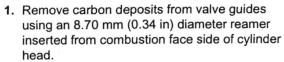

12M3677

1. Remove carbon deposits from valve guides using an 8.70 mm (0.34 in) diameter reamer inserted from combustion face side of cylinder head.
2. Clean valve springs, cotters, caps and valves.
3. Clean inlet valve guide bores. Ensure all loose particles of carbon are removed on completion.
4. Check existing valve stem and head diameters.
5. Check valve stem to guide clearance using new valves.

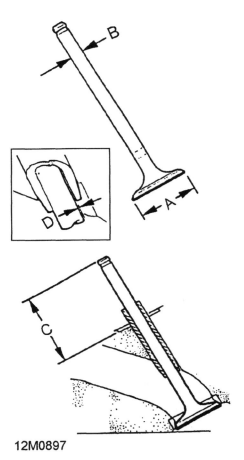

12M0897

6. Renew valves and guides as necessary.
   Valve head diameter **A:**
   Inlet = 39.75 to 40.00 mm (1.5 to 1.6 in)
   Exhaust = 34.226 to 34.48 mm (1.3 to 1.4 in)
   Valve stem diameter **B:**
   Inlet = 8.664 to 8.679 mm (0.341 to 0.342 in)
   Exhaust = 8.651 to 8.666 mm (0.340 to 0.341 in)
7. Check installed height of each valve.
   Valve installed height **C**= 47.63 mm (1.9 in)
8. Renew valve/valve seat insert as necessary.

9. Check valve stem to guide clearance.
   Valve stem to guide clearance **D**:
   Inlet = 0.025 to 0.066 mm (0.001 to 0.002 in)
   Exhaust = 0.038 to 0.078 mm (0.0015 to 0.003 in)
10. Check condition of valve springs:
   Free length = 48.30 mm (1.90 in)
   Fitted length = 40.40 mm (1.60 in)
   Load at fitted length = 339 ± 10 N (76 ± 2 lbf)
   Load at valve open length = 736 ± 22 N (165 ± 2 lbf)

  CAUTION: Valve springs must be replaced as a complete set.

Valve guides - renew

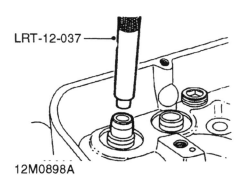

LRT-12-037

12M0898A

1. Using valve guide remover, **LRT-12-037** press valve guide out into combustion face side of cylinder head.

  NOTE: Service valve guides are 0.025mm (0.001 in) oversize on outside diameter to ensure interference fit.

2. Lubricate new valve guide with engine oil and place in position.

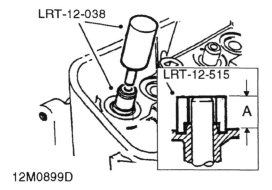

LRT-12-038

LRT-12-515

A

12M0899D

3. Using **LRT-12-038** partially press guide into cylinder head, remove tool.
4. Fit **LRT-12-515** over valve guide and continue to press guide into cylinder head until tool **LRT-12-038** contacts tool **LRT-12-515**. Remove tool.
   Valve guide installed height **A** = 15.0 mm (0.590 in)
5. Ream valve guides to 8.70 mm (0.34 in) diameter. Remove all traces of swarf on completion.

Valve seat inserts - inspection

1. Check valve seat inserts for pitting, burning and wear. Replace inserts as necessary.

Valve seat inserts - renew

 NOTE: Service valve seat inserts are available 0.025 mm (0.001 in) oversize on outside diameter to ensure interference fit.

1. Remove worn valve seats.

 CAUTION: Take care not to damage counterbore in cylinder head.

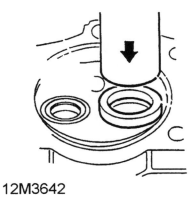

12M3642

2. Heat cylinder head evenly to approximately 120°C (250° F).

 WARNING: Handle hot cylinder head with care.

3. Using a suitable mandrel, press new insert fully into counterbore.
4. Allow cylinder head to air cool.

Valve seats and seat inserts - refacing

⚠ **CAUTION: Renew worn valve guides and seat inserts before refacing valve seats.**

1. Check condition of valve seats and valves that are to be re-used.
2. Remove carbon from valve seats.

 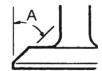

12M0901

3. Reface valves as necessary. If a valve has to be ground to a knife-edge to obtain a true seat, replace valve.
   Valve seating face angle = 45°

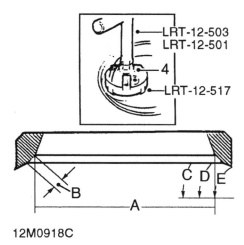

12M0918C

4. Cut valve seats using **LRT-12-501** with **LRT-12-503** and **LRT-12-517** .
   Valve seat:
   Width **A**:
   Inlet = 36.83 mm (1.45 in)
   Exhaust = 31.50 mm (1.24 in)
   Seating width **B**:
   Inlet = 0.89 to 1.4 mm (0.035 to 0.055 in)
   Exhaust = 1.32 to 1.83 mm (0.052 to 0.072 in)
   Angle **C**= 56° to 57°
   Angle **D**= 46° to 46° 25'
   Angle **E**= 20°

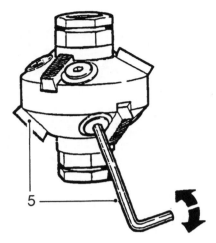

12M0902

5. Ensure cutter blades are correctly fitted to cutter head with angled end of blade downwards, facing work as illustrated. Check that cutter blades are adjusted so that middle of blade contacts area of metal to be cut. Use light pressure and remove minimum amount of material necessary.
6. Remove all traces of swarf on completion.

Valves - lapping-in

1. Lap each valve to its seat using fine grinding paste.
2. Clean valve and seat.

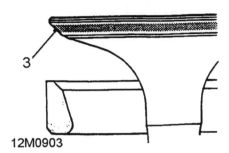

12M0903

3. Coat valve seat with a small quantity of engineer's blue, insert valve and press it into position several times without rotating. Remove valve and check for even and central seating. Seating position shown by engineer's blue should be in centre of valve face.

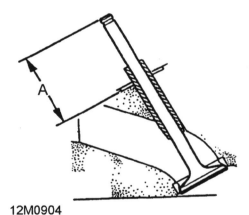

12M0904

4. Check valve installed height if valve seats have been recut or new valves or valve seat inserts have been fitted.
   Valve installed height **A**= 47.63 mm (1.9 in) - maximum
5. Thoroughly clean cylinder head, blow out oilways and coolant passages.

Valves and springs - refit

1. Fit new valve stem oil seals, lubricate valve stems, fit valves, valve springs and caps, compress valve springs using **LRT-12-034** and fit collets.
2. Using a wooden dowel and mallet, lightly tap each valve stem two or three times to seat valve cap and collets.
3. Fit spark plugs and tighten to 20 Nm (15 lbf.ft)

Cylinder head - refit

1. Clean cylinder block faces using a suitable gasket removal spray and plastic scraper; ensure that bolt holes in cylinder block are clean and dry.

⚠ **CAUTION: Do not use metal scraper or machined surfaces may be damaged.**

2. *Engine numbers without suffix B:* Thoroughly clean threads of cylinder head bolts.

⚠ **CAUTION: Cylinder head bolts fitted to engines without suffix B added to serial number are not interchangeable with those fitted to engines with suffix B added to serial number.**

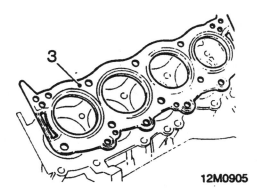

12M0905

3. Fit cylinder head gasket with the word 'TOP' uppermost.

⚠ NOTE: Gasket must be fitted dry.

⚠ **CAUTION: Engines without suffix B have a steel gasket whilst engines with suffix B have a composite gasket. The two types of gasket are not interchangeable and it is essential to ensure that the correct type of gasket is fitted.**

4. Carefully fit cylinder head and locate on dowels.

Engine numbers without suffix B

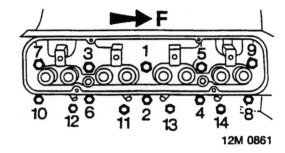

12M 0861

Engine numbers with suffix B

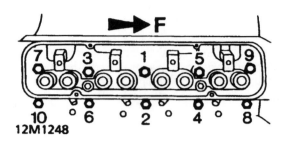

12M1248

 NOTE: RH cylinder head illustrated

5. Lightly oil threads of cylinder head bolts.
6. Fit cylinder head bolts:
   Long bolts: 1, 3 and 5.
   Medium bolts: 2, 4, 6, 7, 8, 9, and 10.
   Short bolts: 11, 12, 13 and 14.
7. Using sequence shown, progressively tighten cylinder head bolts to:
   Bolts 11 to 14 - Outer row - 60 Nm (44 lbf.ft)
   Bolts 2, 4, 6, 8 and 10 - Centre row - 90 Nm (66 lbf.ft)
   Bolts 1, 3, 5, 7 and 9 - Inner row - 90 Nm (66 lbf.ft)

 NOTE: RH cylinder head illustrated

8. Lightly oil threads of new cylinder head bolts.
9. Fit cylinder head bolts:
   Long bolts: 1, 3 and 5
   Short bolts: 2, 4, 6, 7, 8, 9 and 10

 NOTE: There are no bolts fitted in the four lower holes in each cylinder head.

10. Using sequence shown, tighten cylinder head bolts to:
    Stage 1 - 20 Nm (15 lbf.ft)
    Stage 2 - 90°
    Stage 3 - Further 90°

⚠ CAUTION: Do not tighten bolts 180° in one operation.

All engines

11. Fit rocker shaft assembly.

TIMING CHAIN AND GEARS

Distributor - if fitted - remove

1. Remove distributor cap.
2. Rotate crankshaft until centre line of rotor arm is aligned with No. 1 spark plug segment in distributor cap and No. 1 piston is at TDC.

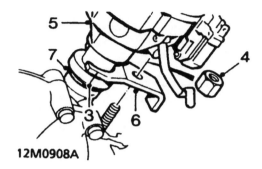

12M0908A

3. Scribe an alignment mark between distributor body and clamp.
4. Remove nut securing distributor clamp.
5. Remove distributor.
6. Remove clamp.
7. Remove and discard 'O' ring from distributor.

Sump - remove

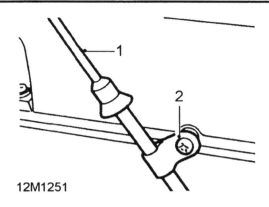

12M1251

1. Remove dipstick.
2. Remove screw securing dipstick tube to LH rocker cover.

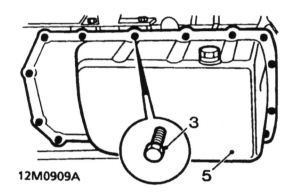

12M0909A

 NOTE: Sump fitted to engines without suffix B engine numbers illustrated.

3. Remove 16 bolts securing sump to cylinder block.

 NOTE: Engine numbers with suffix B, 17 bolts are used to secure sump to cylinder block.

4. Carefully release sump from cylinder block.

 CAUTION: Take care not to damage sealing faces of cylinder block and sump.

5. Remove sump.

Timing cover - remove - Engine numbers without suffix B

1. Remove crankshaft pulley bolt and collect spacer washer.
2. Remove crankshaft pulley.

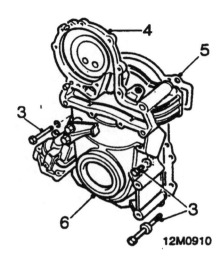

12M0910

3. Remove bolts and nut securing timing cover to cylinder block.
4. Release and remove timing cover.
5. Remove and discard gasket.
6. Remove and discard oil seal from timing cover.

Timing cover - remove - Engine numbers with suffix B

 NOTE: Timing cover, oil pump and oil pressure relief valve are only supplied as an assembly.

1. Using assistance, restrain flywheel and remove crankshaft pulley bolt; collect spacer washer.
2. Remove crankshaft pulley.

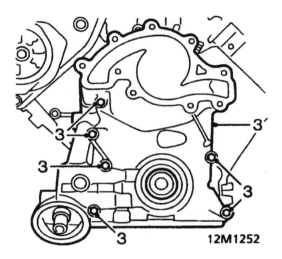

12M1252

3. Noting their fitted position, remove bolts securing timing cover to cylinder block; remove cover.

 NOTE: Dowel located.

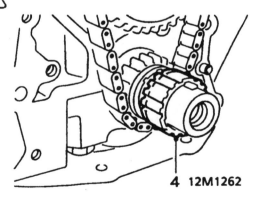

4 12M1262

4. Remove oil pump drive gear.
5. Remove and discard gasket.
6. Remove and discard oil seal from timing cover.

Timing gears - remove

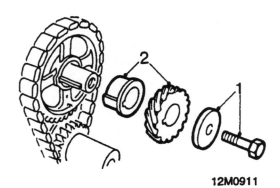

12M0911

1. Restrain camshaft gear and remove bolt securing gear, collect washer.
2. Remove distributor drive gear - if fitted and spacer.

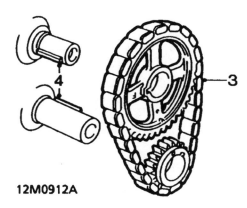

12M0912A

3. Remove timing chain and gears as an assembly.
4. Collect Woodruff keys from camshaft and crankshaft.

Timing chain and gears - inspection

1. Thoroughly clean all components.
2. Inspect distributor drive gear - if fitted for wear.
3. Inspect timing chain links and pins for wear.
4. Inspect timing chain gears for wear. Renew parts as necessary.

Timing gears - refit

1. Clean gear locations on camshaft and crankshaft, fit Woodruff keys.

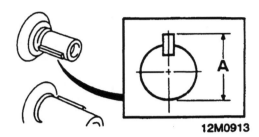

12M0913

2. Check camshaft Woodruff key is fully engaged in keyway.

⚠ **CAUTION: Space between Woodruff key and keyway acts as an oil feed. It is therefore most important that key is properly seated and parallel to axis of camshaft. Overall dimension 'A' must not exceed 30.15 mm (1.2 in).**

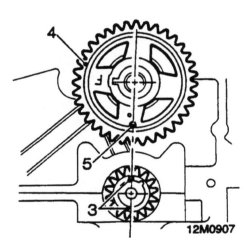

12M0907

3. Temporarily fit crankshaft gear, and if necessary turn crankshaft to bring timing mark on gear to the twelve o'clock position, remove gear.
4. Temporarily fit camshaft gear with marking 'F' facing forwards.
5. Turn camshaft until mark on camshaft gear is at the six o'clock position, remove gear without moving camshaft.

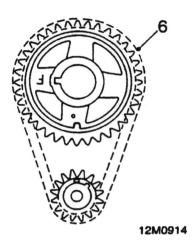

12M0914

6. Position timing gears on work surface with timing marks upwards and aligned.
7. Fit timing chain around gears, keeping timing marks aligned.
8. Fit gear and chain assembly.

△ NOTE: Timing marks and 'F' mark on camshaft gear must be facing forwards.

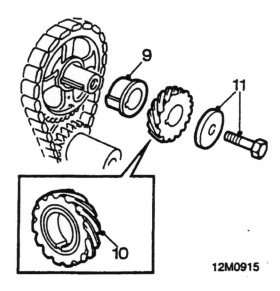

12M0915

9. Fit spacer to camshaft with flange facing forwards.
10. Fit distributor drive gear - if fitted to camshaft with grooved face towards camshaft gear.
11. Fit camshaft gear bolt and washer, restrain camshaft gear and tighten bolt to 50 Nm (37 lbf.ft).

Timing cover - refit - Engine numbers without suffix B

1. Clean sealant from threads of cover bolts.
2. Clean all traces of old gasket material from timing cover and mating face of cylinder block.

⚠ **CAUTION: Use a plastic scraper.**

3. Use a lint free cloth and thoroughly clean oil seal location in timing cover.
4. Lubricate new oil seal sealing surfaces with engine oil.

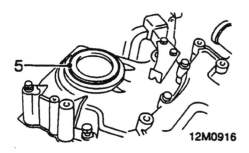

12M0916

5. Locate seal to timing cover and press seal in squarely until flush with front face of timing cover.
6. Position new gasket to cylinder block.
7. Coat threads of timing cover bolts with Loctite 242 sealant.
8. Fit timing cover, fit bolts and nut and tighten progressively to 22 Nm (16 lbf.ft).
9. Fit crankshaft pulley.
10. Fit spacer washer to pulley bolt, fit bolt and tighten to 270 Nm (200 lbf.ft).

Timing cover - refit - Engine numbers with suffix B

 NOTE: Timing cover, oil pump and oil pressure relief valve are only supplied as an assembly.

1. Clean sealant from threads of timing cover bolts.
2. Clean all traces of gasket material from mating faces of timing cover and cylinder block.

 CAUTION: Use a plastic scraper.

3. Clean oil seal location in timing cover.
4. Lubricate oil seal recess in timing cover with engine oil.
5. Apply Hylosil jointing compound to new timing cover gasket, position gasket to cylinder block.
6. Position oil pump drive gear in timing cover with groove towards front of timing cover.

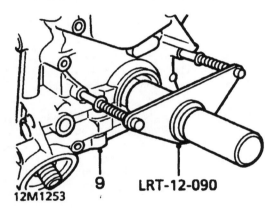

12M1253   9   LRT-12-090

7. Locate tool **LRT-12-090** on timing cover and oil pump drive gear.
8. Position timing cover to cylinder block and at the same time, rotate tool **LRT-12-090** until drive gear keyway is aligned with Woodruff key.
9. Fit timing cover to cylinder block.
10. Smear threads of timing cover bolts with Loctite 242 sealant, fit bolts and tighten progressively to 22 Nm (16 lbf.ft).

 NOTE: Do not fit coolant pump bolts at this stage.

11. Remove tool **LRT-12-090**.

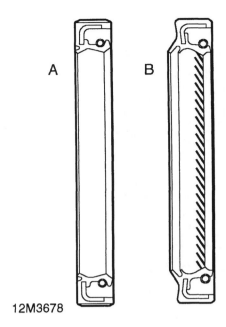

12M3678

A- Early type seal
B- Later type seal - use as replacement for all engines

12. Lubricate new timing cover oil seal with Shell Retinax LX grease ensuring that space between seal lips is filled with grease.

 CAUTION: Do not use any other type of grease.

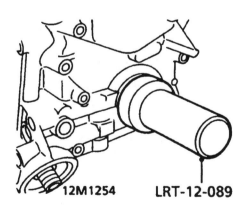

12M1254   LRT-12-089

13. Fit timing cover oil seal using tool **LRT-12-089**.
14. Fit crankshaft pulley, fit bolt and spacer washer; tighten bolt to 270 Nm (200 lbf.ft).

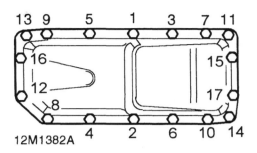

Sump - refit

1. Remove all traces of old sealant from mating faces of cylinder block and sump.

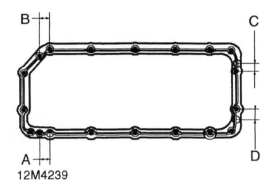

12M4239

12M1382A

⚠ NOTE: Sump fitted to engines with suffix B engine numbers illustrated.

2. Clean mating faces with suitable solvent. Apply a bead of Hylosil type 101 or 106 sealant to sump joint face as shown:
Bead width - areas A, B, C and D = 12 mm (0.5 in)
Bead width - remaining areas = 5 mm (0.20 in)
Bead length - areas A and B = 32 mm (1.23 in)
Bead length - areas C and D = 19 mm (0.75 in)

⚠ CAUTION: Do not spread sealant bead.

3. Fit sump, taking care not to damage sealant bead.

⚠ CAUTION: Sump must be fitted immediately after applying sealant.

4. Fit sump bolts and using sequence shown, tighten progressively to 23 Nm (17 lbf.ft).

⚠ NOTE: Engine numbers without suffix B - use sequence numbers 1 to 8 and 10 to 16.

5. Fit and tighten screw securing dipstick tube to LH rocker cover.
6. Fit dipstick.

Distributor - if fitted - refit

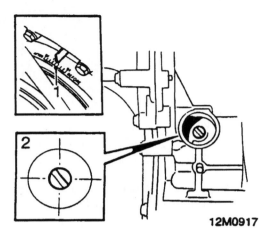

12M0917

1. Ensure timing pointer is aligned with 3° mark on crankshaft pulley and No.1 piston is on the compression stroke.
2. *Engine numbers without suffix B:* Position oil pump drive shaft tongue at the ten to four position.
3. Lubricate a new 'O' ring with engine oil and fit to distributor.

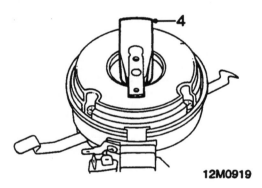

12M0919

4. Turn distributor drive until rotor arm is approximately 30° anti-clockwise from No.1 spark plug segment in distributor cap.
5. Insert distributor into timing cover, engage drive gear and push distributor down until 'O' ring enters bore; position distributor clamp on stud.

6. *Engine numbers without suffix B:* Locate slotted adapter to oil pump drive shaft tongue.
7. Check that centre line of rotor arm is aligned with No.1 spark plug segment in distributor cap and reference marks on distributor body and clamp are aligned; reposition distributor if necessary.
8. Remove rotor arm.
9. Rotate distributor to position pick-up opposite nearest reluctor tooth.

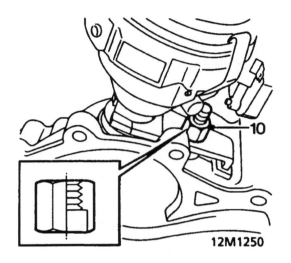

12M1250

10. Fit distributor clamp nut ensuring that counterbored portion is towards clamp; tighten nut to 20 Nm (15 lbf.ft).
11. Fit rotor arm.

⚠ CAUTION: This distributor setting is to enable engine to be started. When engine is refitted, ignition timing must be set using electronic equipment.

OIL COOLER ADAPTER - ENGINE NUMBERS WITHOUT SUFFIX B

Oil cooler adapter - remove

1. Remove oil filter element.

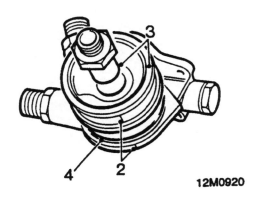

12M0920

2. Mark position of adapter in relation to oil pump cover.
3. Remove centre screw and withdraw adapter.
4. Remove and discard sealing ring.

Oil cooler adapter - refit

1. Thoroughly clean adapter.
2. Position new sealing ring, fit adapter, ensuring marks previously made line up, fit and tighten centre screw.
3. Lubricate sealing ring of oil filter with engine oil.
4. Screw filter on to filter head until it seats then tighten a further half-turn.

OIL PUMP - ENGINE NUMBERS WITHOUT SUFFIX B

Oil pump - remove

1. Remove sump.
2. Remove distributor.
3. Remove timing cover.
4. Remove oil cooler adapter - if fitted.

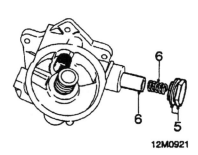

12M0921

5. Remove oil pressure relief valve plug, discard sealing washer.
6. Withdraw pressure relief valve spring and valve.

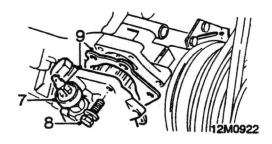

12M0922

7. Remove oil pressure switch, discard sealing washer.
8. Remove bolts securing oil pump cover.
9. Remove cover, remove and discard gasket.
10. Withdraw oil pump gears.

Oil pump - inspection

1. Throughly clean oil pump gear housing, cover and gears.
2. Clean oil pressure relief valve bore in housing.
3. Clean relief valve filter screen.
4. Inspect pump gears for wear and scoring.

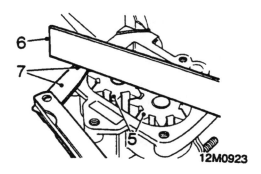

12M0923

5. Fit pump gears into housing.
6. Place straight edge across gears.
7. Check clearance between straight edge and cover face.
   Gear to cover face minimum clearance = 0.05 mm (0.002 in).
   If clearance is below minimum specified check gear recess in housing for wear. Renew housing if necessary.
8. Remove oil pump gears from housing.
9. Clean oil pressure relief valve and spring.
10. Inspect relief valve for wear and scoring.
11. Inspect relief valve spring for wear or signs of collapse.
    Relief spring free length = 81.28 mm (3.2 in)
12. Check relief valve slides freely in its bore with no perceptible side movement.

Oil pump - refit

1. Lubricate relief valve, spring, and bore in housing with clean engine oil.
2. Fit relief valve and valve spring.
3. Fit new sealing washer to plug, fit plug and tighten to 45 Nm (33 lbf.ft).
4. Pack oil pump housing with Petroleum Jelly.

 CAUTION: Use only Petroleum Jelly, no other grease is suitable.

5. Fit oil pump gears ensuring that Petroleum Jelly is forced into every cavity between teeth of gears.

 CAUTION: Unless pump is fully packed with Petroleum Jelly it may not prime itself when the engine is started.

6. Fit new pump cover gasket.
7. Position cover, fit bolts and tighten progressively to 12 Nm (9 lbf.ft).
8. Fit oil cooler adapter.
9. Fit timing cover.
10. Fit distributor.
11. Fit sump.

OIL PUMP - ENGINE NUMBERS WITH SUFFIX B

⚠ **CAUTION: Overhaul procedures for the oil pump and oil pressure relief valve are limited to carrying out dimensional checks. In the event of wear or damage being found, a replacement timing cover assembly must be fitted.**

Oil pump - remove

1. Remove timing cover.

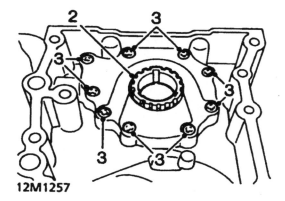

12M1257

2. Remove oil pump drive gear.
3. Remove screws and bolt - if fitted securing cover plate, remove plate.

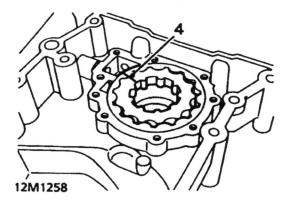

12M1258

4. Make suitable alignment marks on inner and outer rotors, remove rotors.

Oil pressure relief valve - remove

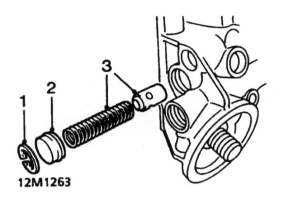

12M1263

1. Remove circlip.
2. Remove relief valve plug, remove and discard 'O' ring.
3. Remove relief valve spring and piston.

Oil pump - inspection

1. Thoroughly clean oil pump drive gear, cover plate, rotors and housing. Remove all traces of Loctite from cover plate securing screws; ensure tapped holes in timing cover are clean and free from oil.
2. Check mating surfaces of cover plate, rotors and housing for scoring.

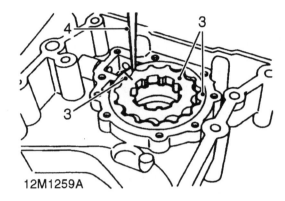

12M1259A

3. Assemble rotors and oil pump drive gear in housing ensuring that reference marks are aligned.
4. Using feeler gauges, check clearance between teeth of inner and outer rotors:
   Maximum clearance = 0.25 mm (0.01 in)

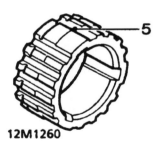

12M1260

5. Remove oil pump drive gear, check depth of any wear steps on gear teeth:
   Wear step maximum depth = 0.15 mm (0.006 in)

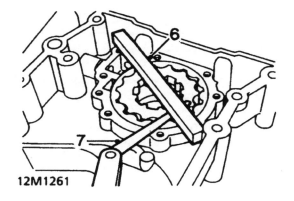

12M1261

6. Place a straight edge across housing.
7. Using feeler gauges, check clearance between
straight edge and rotors:
Maximum clearance = 0.1 mm (0.004 in)

Oil pressure relief valve - inspection

1. Clean relief valve components and piston bore
in timing cover.
2. Check piston and bore for scoring and that
piston slides freely in bore with no perceptible
side movement.
3. Check relief valve spring for damage and
distortion; check spring free length:
Spring free length = 60.0 mm (2.4 in)

Oil pump - refit

1. Lubricate rotors, oil pump drive gear, cover plate and housing with engine oil.
2. Assemble rotors in housing ensuring that reference marks are aligned.
3. Position cover plate to housing.
4. Apply Loctite 222 to threads of cover plate screws and bolt - if fitted, fit but do not fully tighten screws and bolt.
5. Position drive gear in oil pump, tighten cover plate screws and bolt - if fitted to:
   Screws - 4 Nm (3 lbf.ft).
   Bolt - 8 Nm (6 lbf.ft)
6. Fit timing cover.

Oil pressure relief valve - refit

1. Lubricate new 'O' ring with engine oil and fit to relief valve plug.
2. Lubricate relief valve spring, piston and piston bore with engine oil.
3. Assemble piston to relief valve spring, insert piston and spring into piston bore.
4. Fit relief valve plug, depress plug and fit circlip.
5. Ensure circlip is fully seated in groove.

CAMSHAFT AND TAPPETS

Camshaft end-float - check

⚠ NOTE: this check is only applicable to camshafts fitted with thrust plate.

1. Remove rocker shaft assemblies.
2. Remove push rods and store in fitted order.
3. Remove timing chain and gears.

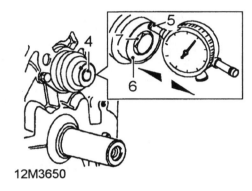

12M3650

4. Temporarily fit camshaft gear bolt.
5. Attach a suitable DTI to front of cylinder block with stylus of gauge contacting end of camshaft.
6. Push camshaft rearwards and zero gauge.
7. Using camshaft gear bolt, pull camshaft forwards and note end-float reading on gauge. End-float = 0.05 to 0.35 mm (0.002 to 0.014 in)

8. if end-float is incorrect, fit a new thrust plate and re-check. If end-float is still incorrect, a new camshaft must be fitted.

Camshaft and tappets - remove

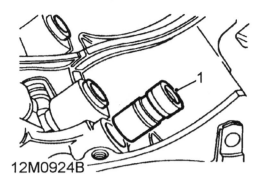

12M0924B

1. Remove tappets and retain with their respective push rods.

⚠ NOTE: If tappets cannot be removed due to damaged camshaft contact area, proceed as follows:

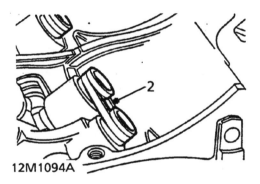

12M1094A

2. Lift tappets in pairs to the point where damaged face is about to enter tappet bore and fit rubber bands to retain tappets. Repeat until all tappets are retained clear of camshaft lobes. The tappets can then be withdrawn out the bottom of their bores when the sump and camshaft are removed.

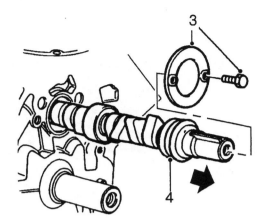

12M0925B

3. Remove 2 bolts securing camshaft thrust plate - if fitted to cylinder block, remove plate.
4. Withdraw camshaft, taking care not to damage bearings in cylinder block.

Camshaft and tappets - inspection

1. Throughly clean all components.
2. Inspect camshaft bearing journals and lobes for signs of wear, pitting, scoring and overheating.
3. Support camshaft front and rear bearings on vee blocks, and using a DTI, measure camshaft run-out on centre bearing. Maximum permitted run-out = 0.05 mm (0.002 in).
4. Inspect camshaft thrust plate - if fitted, for wear, replace plate if wear is evident.
5. Clean and inspect tappets. Check for an even, circular wear pattern on the camshaft contact area. If contact area is pitted or a square wear pattern has developed, tappet must be renewed.
6. Inspect tappet body for excessive wear or scoring. Replace tappet if scoring or deep wear patterns extend up to oil feed area. Clean and inspect tappet bores in engine block.
7. Ensure that tappets rotate freely in their respective bores.
8. Inspect push rod contact area of tappet, replace tappet if surface is rough or pitted.

Camshaft and tappets - refit

1. Lubricate camshaft journals with clean engine oil and carefully insert camshaft into cylinder block.
2. Fit camshaft thrust plate - if fitted, ensuring that it is correctly located in camshaft groove. Fit bolts and tighten to 25 Nm (18 lbf.ft)

 NOTE: If camshaft or thrust plate has been replaced, it will be necessary to re-check camshaft end-float.

3. Immerse tappets in clean engine oil. Before fitting, pump the inner sleeve of tappet several times using a push rod, to prime tappet and reduce tappet noise when engine is first started.
4. Lubricate tappet bores with clean engine oil and fit tappets in removed order.

 NOTE: Some tappet noise may be evident on initial start-up. If necessary, run the engine at 2500 rev/min for a few minutes until noise ceases.

5. Fit timing chain and gears.
6. Fit rocker shaft assemblies.

PISTONS, CONNECTING RODS, PISTON RINGS AND CYLINDER BORES

Pistons and connecting rods - remove

1. Remove cylinder head(s).
2. Remove big-end bearings.
3. Remove carbon ridge from top of each cylinder bore.
4. Suitably identify each piston to its respective cylinder bore.
5. Push connecting rod and piston assembly to top of cylinder bore and withdraw assembly.
6. Repeat above procedure for remaining pistons.

 CAUTION: Big-end bearing shells must be replaced whenever they are removed.

Piston rings - remove

1. Using a suitable piston ring expander, remove and discard piston rings.
2. Remove carbon from piston ring grooves.

 NOTE: Use an old broken piston ring with a squared off end.

 CAUTION: Do not use a wire brush.

Piston rings - inspection

1. Temporarily fit new compression rings to piston.

 NOTE: The ring marked 'TOP' must be fitted, with marking uppermost, into second groove. The chrome ring fits into top groove and can be fitted either way round.

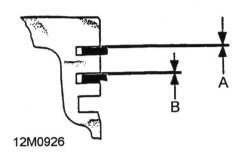

12M0926

2. Check compression ring to groove clearance:
   Top compression ring **A** = 0.05 to 0.10 mm (0.002 to 0.004 in)
   2nd compression ring **B** = 0.05 to 0.10 mm (0.002 to 0.004 in)

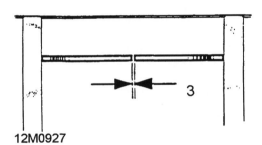

12M0927

3. Insert piston ring into its relevant cylinder bore, held square to bore with piston and check ring gaps.
   Top compression ring = 0.44 to 0.57 mm (0.02 to 0.22 in)
   2nd compression ring = 0.44 to 0.57 mm(0.02 to 0.22 in)
   Oil control ring rails = 0.38 to 1.40 mm (0.14 to 0.05 in)

Pistons - remove

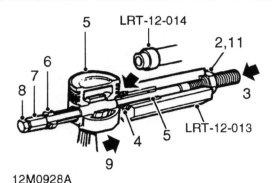

12M0928A

1. Clamp hexagon body of **LRT-12-013** in vice.
2. Screw large nut back until flush with end of centre screw.
3. Push centre screw forward until nut contacts thrust race.
4. Locate piston adapter **LRT-12-014** with its long spigot inside bore of hexagon body.
5. Locate piston and connecting rod assembly on centre screw and up to adapter **LRT-12-014.**
6. Fit remover/replacer bush of **LRT-12-014** on centre screw with flanged end away from gudgeon pin.
7. Screw stop nut on to centre screw.
8. Lock the stop nut securely with lockscrew.
9. Push connecting rod to right to locate end of gudgeon pin in adapter **LRT-12-014.**
10. Ensure remover/replacer is located in gudgeon pin bore of piston.
11. Screw large nut up to **LRT-12-013.**
12. Hold lockscrew and turn large nut until gudgeon pin is withdrawn from piston.
13. Dismantle tool and remove piston, connecting rod and gudgeon pin.

 NOTE: Keep each piston and gudgeon pin with their respective connecting rod.

14. Repeat above operation for remaining pistons.

Pistons and connecting rods - inspection

1. Clean carbon from pistons
2. Inspect pistons for distortion and cracks.

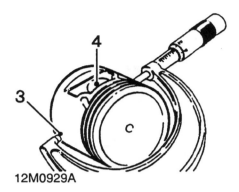

12M0929A

3. Measure piston diameter at 90° to gudgeon pin axis and 10 mm (0.4 in) from bottom of skirt. The piston must be 0.02 mm to 0.045 mm (0.001 to 0.002 in) smaller than cylinder bore.
4. Check gudgeon pin bore in piston for signs of overheating.
5. Check connecting rods for alignment.

Gudgeon pins - inspection

 NOTE: Gudgeon pins are only supplied as an assembly with replacement pistons.

1. Check gudgeon pins for signs of wear and overheating.
2. Check clearance of gudgeon pin in piston:
   Gudgeon pin to piston clearance = 0.006 to 0.015 mm (0.0002 to 0.0006 in)
3. Check overall dimensions of gudgeon pin:
   Overall length = 72.67 to 72.79 mm (2.85 to 2.86 in)
   Diameter - measured at each end and centre of pin = 22.215 to 22.220 mm (0.87 to 0.871 in)

Cylinder liner bore - inspection

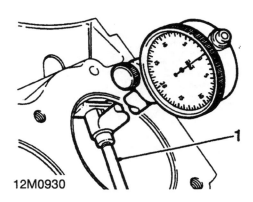

12M0930

1. Measure cylinder bore wear in two axis 40 to 50 mm (1.5 to 1.9 in) from top of bore:
   Cylinder bore diameter - standard:
   3.5 litre = 88.90 mm (3.5 in)
   3.9 litre = 94.00 mm (3.7 in)
   4.2 litre = 94.00 mm (3.7 in)
   Maximum ovality = 0.013 mm (0.0005 in)
2. Compare cylinder bore diameter with piston diameter and calculate piston to cylinder bore clearance.
   Piston to cylinder bore clearance = 0.002 to 0.045 mm (0.001 to 0.002 in)

NOTE: Pistons are available in service standard size and 0.508 mm (0.02 in) oversize. Service standard size pistons are supplied 0.0254 mm (0.01 in) oversize. When fitting new service standard size pistons, check for correct piston to bore clearance, rebore or hone bore if necessary.

CAUTION: The temperature of piston and cylinder block must be the same to ensure accurate measurement. When reboring cylinder block, the crankshaft main bearing caps must be fitted and bolts tightened to:
Initial torque - all bearing caps - 13 Nm (10 lbf.ft)
Numbers 1 to 4 bearing caps - 70 Nm (52 lbf.ft).
Rear bearing cap - 90 Nm (66 lbf.ft).

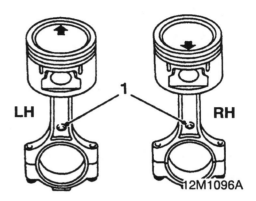

3. If only new piston rings are to be fitted, break cylinder bore glazing using a fine grit, to produce a 60° cross-hatch finish.

⚠ **CAUTION: Ensure all traces of grit are removed after above operation. If dipstick tube has been removed, coat portion of tube below collar with Loctite 572 prior to refitting.**

Pistons - refit

⚠ **CAUTION: On later 4.2L engines the piston has a 0.5 mm (0.02 in) offset gudgeon pin which can be identified by an arrow mark on the piston crown. This arrow MUST always point to the front of the engine.**

LH   1   RH

12M1096A

1. *4.2L engine only:* Assemble pistons to connecting rods with arrow on piston pointing towards domed shaped boss on connecting rod for RH bank of cylinders, and arrow pointing away from dome shaped boss for LH bank of cylinders.

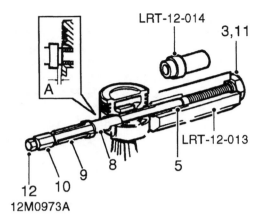

LRT-12-014
3,11
A
LRT-12-013
12 10 9 8 5
12M0973A

15. Dismantle tool, remove piston, check no damage has occurred during pressing and piston moves freely on gudgeon pin.
16. Repeat above operation for remaining pistons.

2. Clamp hexagon body of **LRT-12-013** in vice.
3. Slacken large nut and pull the centre screw 50 mm (1.9 in) out of hexagon body.
4. Locate piston adapter **LRT-12-014** with its long spigot inside bore of hexagon body.
5. Fit parallel sleeve, grooved end last, up to shoulder on centre screw.
6. Lubricate gudgeon pin and bores of connecting rod and piston with graphited oil.
7. Locate connecting rod and piston to centre screw with connecting rod entered on sleeve up to groove.
8. Fit gudgeon pin on to centre screw and into piston bore up to connecting rod.
9. Fit remover/replacer bush with flanged end towards gudgeon pin.
10. Screw the stop nut on to centre screw and position piston against face of adapter **LRT-12-014**.
11. Lubricate centre screw threads and thrust race with graphited oil, screw large nut up to thrust race.
12. Lock the stop nut securely with lockscrew.
13. Set torque wrench to 16 Nm (12 lbf.ft), and using a socket on large nut, pull gudgeon pin in until flange of remover/replacer bush is distance **A** from face of piston.
Distance **A** = 0.4 mm (0.02 in)
14. If correct torque figure is not achieved during above operation, fit of gudgeon pin to connecting rod is not acceptable and necessitates renewal of components.

⚠ **CAUTION: The centre screw and thrust race must be kept well lubricated throughout operation. Flange of remover/replacer must not be allowed to contact piston.**

Piston to cylinder bore clearance - checking

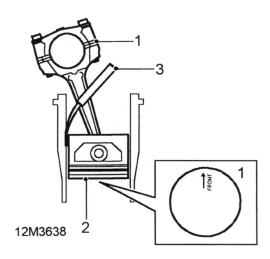

12M3638

1. Starting with number 1 piston, invert piston and with arrow on piston crown pointing towards REAR of cylinder block, insert piston in cylinder liner.
2. Position piston with bottom of skirt 30 mm (1.2 in) from top of cylinder block.
3. Using feeler gauges, measure and record clearance between piston and left hand side of cylinder block:
   Piston to bore clearance = 0.02 to 0.045 mm (0.001 to 0.002 in)
4. Repeat above procedures for remaining pistons.

Pistons and connecting rods - refit

1. Fit oil control ring rails and expander, ensuring ends butt and not overlap.

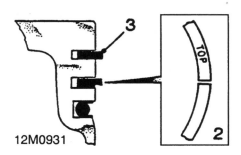

12M0931

2. Fit ring marked 'TOP' with marking uppermost into second groove.
3. Fit top compression ring into groove either way round.

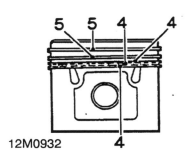

12M0932

4. Position oil control expander ring joint and ring rail gaps all at one side, between gudgeon pin and away from left hand side of piston - viewed from front of piston. Space gaps in ring rails approximately 25 mm (1.0 in) each side of expander ring joint.
5. Position compression rings with ring gaps on opposite sides of piston between gudgeon pin and right hand side of piston - viewed from front of piston.
6. Thoroughly clean cylinder bores.
7. Lubricate piston rings and gudgeon pin with engine oil.
8. Lubricate cylinder bores with engine oil.

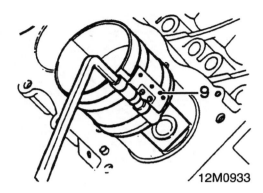

12M0933

9. Fit ring clamp to piston and compress piston rings.
10. Insert connecting rod and piston assembly into respective cylinder bore ensuring domed shaped boss on connecting rod faces towards front of engine on RH bank of cylinders, and towards rear on LH bank of cylinders.

⚠ NOTE: When both connecting rods are fitted to each journal, bosses will face towards each other.

11. Fit big-end bearing caps and bearing shells.
12. Fit cylinder head(s).

FLYWHEEL AND STARTER RING GEAR

Flywheel - remove

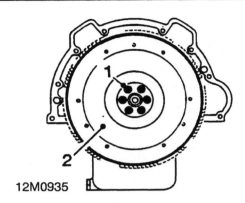

12M0935

1. Restrain crankshaft and remove 6 bolts securing flywheel.
2. Remove flywheel.

⚠ NOTE: Dowel located.

Flywheel and starter ring gear - inspection

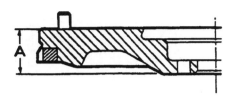

12M0936

1. Inspect flywheel face for cracks, scores and overheating. The flywheel can be refaced providing thickness does not go below minimum.
   Flywheel minimum thickness **A** = 39.93 mm (1.6 in)
2. Inspect ring gear for worn, chipped and broken teeth.

 CAUTION: Do not attempt to remove reluctor ring - if fitted.

3. Renew ring gear if necessary.

Starter ring gear - renew

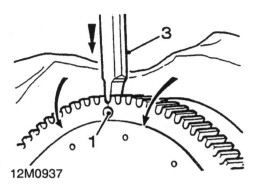

12M0937

1. Drill a 9.5 mm (0.375 in) diameter hole axially at base of tooth and inner diameter of starter ring, sufficiently deep enough to weaken ring gear.

 CAUTION: Do not allow drill to enter flywheel.

2. Secure flywheel in soft jawed vice.
3. Split ring gear using a cold chisel.

 WARNING: Wear safety goggles and take precautions against flying fragments when splitting ring gear.

4. Remove flywheel from vice, remove old ring gear, and place flywheel, clutch side down, on a flat surface.

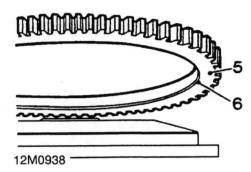

12M0938

Flywheel - refit

1. Fit flywheel and locate on 2 dowels.
2. Fit flywheel bolts.
3. Using assistance, restrain crankshaft and tighten flywheel bolts to 80 Nm (59 lbf.ft).

5. Heat new ring gear uniformly to between 170° and 175° C (340° and 350° F).

 CAUTION: Do not exceed this temperature.

 WARNING: Handle hot ring gear with care.

6. Locate ring gear on flywheel with chamfered inner diameter towards flywheel flange.

 NOTE: If ring gear is chamfered on both sides, it can be fitted either way round.

7. Press ring gear on to flywheel until it butts against flywheel flange.
8. Allow flywheel to air cool.

DRIVE PLATE AND RING GEAR ASSEMBLY

Drive plate and ring gear assembly - remove

1. Suitably identify each component to its fitted position.

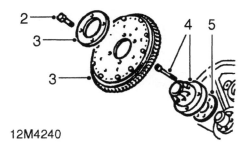

12M4240

 NOTE: Shimmed drive plate assembly illustrated.

2. Remove 4 bolts securing drive plate assembly.
3. Remove buttress ring and drive plate assembly.

 NOTE: Dowel located.

4. Remove 6 socket head Allen screws securing hub aligner to crankshaft, remove hub aligner.
5. Remove selective shim - if fitted; retain shim.

Drive plate and ring gear - inspection

1. Inspect drive plate for cracks and distortion.
2. Renew drive plate if necessary.
3. Inspect ring gear for worn, chipped and broken teeth.
4. Renew ring gear assembly if necessary.

Drive plate and ring gear assembly - check setting height

⚠ NOTE: The following procedures are only applicable to shimmed drive plates, there is no need to check setting height on drive plates which are not shimmed.

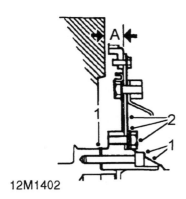

12M1402

1. Fit original selective shim and hub aligner, fit socket head Allen screws and tighten to 80 Nm (63 lbf.ft).
2. Fit drive plate assembly and buttress ring ensuring that reference marks are aligned; fit bolts and tighten to 45 Nm (33 lbf.ft).

⚠ CAUTION: If a new drive plate assembly is being fitted, paint mark on plate must face towards torque converter.

3. Check the setting height:
   Drive plate setting height **A** = 8.08 to 8.20 mm (0.32 to 0.33 in)
4. If setting height is not as specified, remove buttress ring, drive plate assembly, hub aligner and selective shim.

5. Measure existing shim and, if necessary, select appropriate shim to obtain specified setting height.
   Shims available:
   1.20 - 1.25mm (0.048 to 0.050 in)
   1.30 - 1.35mm (0.051 to 0.053 in)
   1.40 - 1.45mm (0.055 to 0.057 in)
   1.50 - 1.55mm (0.059 to 0.061 in)
   1.60 - 1.65mm (0.063 to 0.065 in)
   1.70 - 1.75mm (0.067 to 0.070 in)
   1.80 - 1.85mm (0.071 to 0.073 in)
   1.90 - 1.95mm (0.075 to 0.077 in)
   2.00 - 2.05mm (0.079 to 0.081 in)
   2.10 - 2.15mm (0.083 to 0.085 in)

6. Retain selected shim

Drive plate and ring gear assembly - refit

1. Position selected shim - if fitted to crankshaft.
2. Fit hub aligner, fit Allen screws and tighten to 85 Nm (63 lbf.ft).
3. Fit drive plate assembly and buttress ring ensuring that reference marks are aligned or that paint mark is towards torque converter.
4. Fit bolts and tighten to 45 Nm (33 lbf.ft).

CRANKSHAFT, MAIN AND BIG-END BEARINGS

Big-end bearings - remove

1. Remove sump.

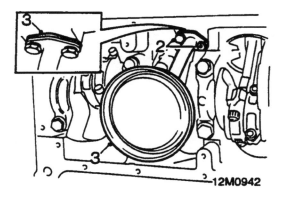

12M0942

2. Remove 2 bolts securing oil strainer.
3. Remove strainer, remove and discard gasket.
4. Suitably identify bearing caps to their respective connecting rods.

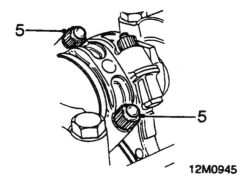

12M0945

5. Remove 2 nuts/bolts securing each bearing cap.
6. Remove bearing cap, remove and discard bearing shell.

 CAUTION: Keep bearing caps and nuts/bolts in their fitted order.

7. *Bolts fitted in connecting rods:* Fit a length of plastic tubing over each connecting rod bolt.
8. Push each piston up its respective bore, remove and discard shells from connecting rods.

 NOTE: Big-end bearing shells must be replaced whenever they are removed.

Big-end bearings - refit

1. Fit new bearing shells to each connecting rod.

 NOTE: Big-end bearings are available in 0.254 and 0.508 mm (0.01 and 0.02 in) oversizes.

2. Lubricate bearing shells and crankshaft journals with engine oil.
3. Pull connecting rods on to crankshaft journals and remove plastic tubing from bolts - if fitted.
4. Fit new bearing shells to each big-end bearing cap.

 NOTE: If crankshaft has been reground, ensure appropriate oversize bearing shells are fitted.

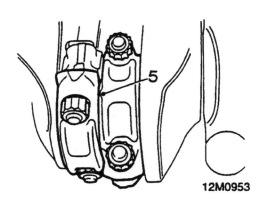

12M0953

5. Lubricate bearing shells and fit bearing caps ensuring reference marks on connecting rods and bearing caps are aligned.

 NOTE: Rib on edge of bearing cap must face towards front of engine on RH bank of cylinders and towards rear on LH bank of cylinders.

6. Fit bearing cap nuts/bolts and tighten to 50 Nm (37 lbf.ft).
7. Check connecting rods move freely sideways on crankshaft. Tightness indicates insufficient bearing clearance or misaligned connecting rod.

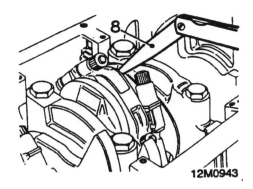

12M0943

8. Check clearance between connecting rods on each crankshaft journal.
Connecting rod clearance = 0.15 to 0.37 mm (0.006 to 0.01 in).
9. Clean oil strainer.
10. Clean gasket mating faces on strainer and cylinder block.
11. Fit gasket to strainer, position strainer, fit bolts and tighten to 10 Nm (7 lbf.ft).
12. Fit sump.

Crankshaft - remove

1. Remove flywheel or drive plate and ring gear assembly.
2. Remove timing cover.
3. Remove timing gears.
4. Remove big-end bearings.

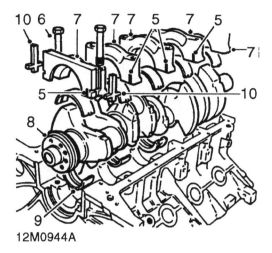

12M0944A

5. Make suitable reference marks between each main bearing cap and cylinder block.
6. Starting at centre main bearing and working outwards, progressively slacken then remove 10 main bearing cap bolts.

 CAUTION: Keep bolts in their fitted order.

7. Remove 5 main bearing caps and bearing shells, discard shells.
8. Lift out crankshaft and rear oil seal. Remove and discard oil seal.
9. Remove and discard 5 bearing shells from cylinder block.

 NOTE: Main bearing shells must be replaced whenever they are removed.

10. Remove and discard side seals from rear main bearing cap.
11. Remove Woodruff key from crankshaft.

Crankshaft - inspection

1. Clean crankshaft and blow out oil passages.

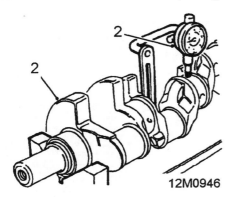

12M0946

2. Support crankshaft front and rear bearing journals on vee blocks, and using a DTI, measure run-out on centre main bearing. Maximum permitted run-out = 0.08 mm (0.003 in)
   If run-out exceeds permitted maximum, crankshaft is unsuitable for regrinding and should be replaced.

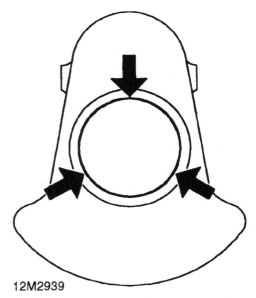

12M2939

3. Measure each journal for overall wear and ovality, make 3 checks at 120° intervals.
   Main bearing journal diameter = 58.409 to 58.422 mm (2.29 to 2.30 in)
   Maximum out of round = 0.040 mm (0.002 in)
   Big-end bearing journal diameter = 50.800 to 50.812 mm (1.99 to 2.00 in)
   Maximum out of round = 0.040 mm (0.002 in)
   If measurements exceed permitted maximum, regrind or fit new crankshaft.

⚠ NOTE: Crankshaft main bearings are available in 0.254 and 0.508 mm (0.01 and 0.02 in) oversizes. When fitting 0.508 mm (0.02 in) oversize bearings, centre main bearing, which controls crankshaft end-float, has thrust faces increased in thickness by 0.254 mm (0.01 in). Therefore if 0.508 mm (0.02 in) oversize bearings are to be fitted, 0.127 mm (0.005 in) must be machined off each thrust face of centre main bearing shell to achieve correct end-float. Ensure an equal amount of material is removed from each thrust face.

Crankshaft dimensions:

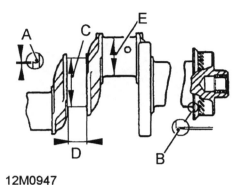

12M0947

Bearing journal radius - all journals except rear main journal **A** = 1.90 to 2.28 mm (0.075 to 0.09 in).
Rear main bearing journal radius **B** = 3.04 mm (0.012 in)

Bearing journal diameter **C** :
Standard = 58.409 to 58.422mm (2.29 to 2.3 in).
0.254 mm (0.01 in) undersize = 58.154 to 58.168 mm (2.290 to 2.300 in)
0.508 mm (0.02 in)undersize = 57.900 to 57.914 mm (2.280 to 2.281 in)

Bearing journal width **D** = 26.975 to 27.026 mm (1.062 to 1.064 in).

Bearing journal diameter **E** :
Standard = 50.800 to 50.812 mm (1.99 to 2.00 in).
0.254 mm (0.01 in) undersize = 50.546 to 50.558 mm (1.98 to 1.99 in)
0.508 mm (0.02 in) undersize = 50.292 to 50.305 mm (1.97 to 1.98 in)

1. Check crankshaft spigot bearing for wear, replace if necessary:
   Spigot bearing inside diameter = 19.177 + 0.025 - 0.000 mm (0.75 + 0.001 - 0.000 in)

Crankshaft spigot bearing - renew

1. Carefully extract old spigot bearing.
2. Clean bearing recess in crankshaft.

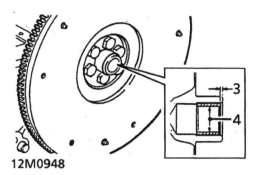

12M0948

3. Fit new bearing flush with, or to a maximum of 1.6 mm (0.06 in) below end face of crankshaft.
4. Ream bearing to correct inside diameter.
   Spigot bearing inside diameter = 19.177 + 0.025 - 0.000 mm (0.75 + 0.001 - 0.000 in)
5. Remove all traces of swarf.

Crankshaft - refit

1. Clean main bearing caps, bearing shell recesses and mating surfaces of cylinder block.

 CAUTION: Ensure main bearing cap bolt holes in cylinder block are clean and dry.

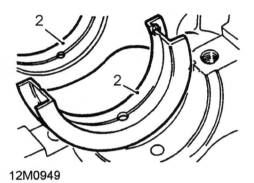

12M0949

2. Fit new upper main bearing shells, with oil holes and grooves, in cylinder block, ensuring flanged shell is fitted in centre position.
3. Lubricate main bearing shells with engine oil and position crankshaft in cylinder block.
4. Fit new main bearing shells to bearing caps and lubricate with engine oil.
5. Lubricate main bearing shells and fit numbers 1 to 4 bearing caps ensuring reference marks made during dismantling are aligned.
6. Fit numbers 1 to 4 main bearing cap bolts and tighten to 13 Nm (10 lbf.ft).

 CAUTION: Do not tighten bolts further at this stage.

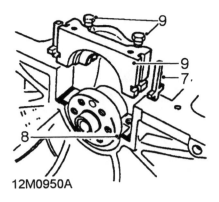

12M0950A

7. Fit side seals to rear main bearing cap.

 CAUTION: Seals must protrude approximately 1.5 mm (0.05 in) above bearing cap face.

8. Apply a 3 mm (0.12 in) wide bead of Hylomar PL32 jointing compound to bearing cap rear mating face on cylinder block.

 CAUTION: Ensure sealant does not enter bolt holes.

9. Lubricate rear main bearing shell and side seals with engine oil, fit bearing cap assembly.
10. Fit rear main bearing cap bolts and tighten to 13 Nm (10 lbf.ft).

 CAUTION: Do not tighten bolts further at this stage.

11. Clean seal location and running surface on crankshaft.
12. *Engine numbers without suffix B:* Clean seal protector **LRT-12-010** and lubricate with engine oil.
13. *Engine numbers with suffix B:* Clean seal protector **LRT-12-095** and lubricate with engine oil.
14. Lubricate oil seal lip with engine oil.

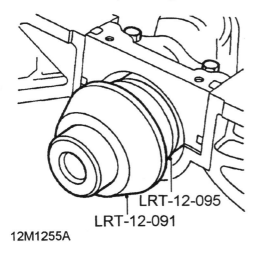

LRT-12-095
LRT-12-091
12M1255A

 NOTE: Seal protector LRT-12-095 illustrated.

15. Position seal protector to crankshaft.
16. *Engine numbers without suffix B:* Fit oil seal squarely using hand pressure only until fully seated in recess.
17. *Engine numbers with suffix B:* Fit seal using tool **LRT-12-091.**

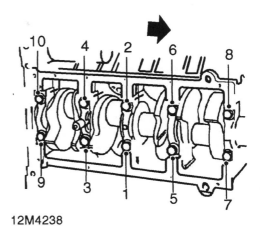

12M4238

18. Using sequence shown, tighten main bearing cap bolts to:
    Numbers 1 to 4 bearing caps - 70 Nm (52 lbf.ft)
    Rear bearing cap -90 Nm (66 lbf.ft)

19. Fit Woodruff key to crankshaft.
20. Check crankshaft end-float.

⚠ **NOTE: If 0.508 mm (0.02 in) oversize main bearings have been fitted, it may be necessary to machine thrust faces of centre main bearing to achieve correct end-float. Ensure an equal amount of material is removed from each thrust face.**

21. Fit big-end bearings.
22. Fit timing cover and gears.
23. Fit flywheel or drive plate and ring gear assembly.

Crankshaft end - float - check

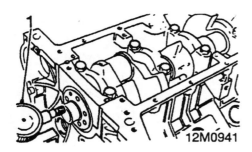

1. Set-up DTI to measure end float.
2. Move crankshaft forwards and zero gauge.
3. Move crankshaft rearwards, record end-float
   reading obtained.
   Crankshaft end-float = 0.10 to 0.20mm (0.004
   to 0.008 in).
4. Remove DTI.

 NOTE: Crankshaft end-float is controlled
by thrust faces on upper half of centre
main bearing shell.

Distributed by Brooklands Books Ltd., PO Box 146, Cobham,
Surrey, KT11 1LG, England Phone: 01932 865051 Fax: 01932 868803
E-mail: sales@brooklands-books.com

ISBN 9781855205284   Part No. LRL 0164ENG
Printed in England   Ref: LRP3WH

LAND ROVER 4.0 & 4.6 LITRE V8 ENGINE OVERHAUL MANUAL

These engines having Serial No. Prefix 42D, 46D, 47D, 48D, 50D or 51D are fitted to the following models:

New Range Rover

Discovery - North American Specification - 1996 MY Onwards

Defender- North American Specification - 1997 MY Onwards

Defender V8i Automatic

Publication Part No. LRL 0164ENG
Published by Land Rover Limited
© 1997 Copyright Land Rover Limited

INTRODUCTION

How to use this Manual

To assist in the use of this Manual the section title is given at the top and the relevant sub-section is given at the bottom of each page.

This manual contains procedures for overhaul of the V8 engine on the bench with the gearbox, clutch, inlet manifold, exhaust manifolds, coolant pump, starter motor, alternator, and all other ancillary equipment removed. For information regarding General Information, Adjustments, removal of oil seals, engine units and ancillary equipment, consult the Repair Manual.

This manual is divided into 3 sections:
• Data, Torque & Tools
• Description and Operation and
• Overhaul

To assist filing of revised information each sub-section is numbered from page 1.

Individual items are to be overhauled in the sequence in which they appear in this manual. Items numbers in the illustrations are referred to in the text.

Overhaul operations include reference to Service tool numbers and the associated illustration depicts the tool. Where usage is not obvious the tool is shown in use. Land Rover tool numbers are quoted, for the equivalent Rover Cars tool number refer to the Service Tool section. Operations also include reference to wear limits, relevant data, and specialist information and useful assembly details.

WARNINGS, CAUTIONS and **NOTES** have the following meanings:

 WARNING: Procedures which must be followed precisely to avoid the possibility of injury.

 CAUTION: Calls attention to procedures which must be followed to avoid damage to components.

 NOTE: Gives helpful information.

Engine serial number

The engine serial number and conpression ratio will be found stamped on a cast pad on the cylinder block between numbers 3 and 5 cylinders. The compression ratio is above the serial number.

References

With the engine and gearbox assembly removed, the crankshaft pulley end of the engine is referred to as the front. References to RH and LH banks of cylinders are taken viewing from the flywheel end of the engine.

Operations covered in this Manual do not include reference to testing the vehicle after repair. It is essential that work is inspected and tested after completion and if necessary a road test of the vehicle is carried out particularly where safety related items are concerned.

Dimensions

The dimensions quoted are to design engineering specification with Service Limits where applicable.

REPAIRS AND REPLACEMENTS

When replacement parts are required it is essential that only Land Rover recommended parts are used.

Attention is particularly drawn to the following points concerning repairs and the fitting of replacement parts and accessories.

Torque wrench setting figures given in this Manual must be used. Locking devices, where specified, must be fitted. If the efficiency of a locking device is impaired during removal it must be renewed.

The terms of the vehicle warranty may be invalidated by the fitting of parts other than Land Rover recommended parts. All Land Rover recommended parts have the full backing of the vehicle warranty.

Land Rover dealers are obliged to supply only Land Rover recommended parts.

SPECIFICATION

Land Rover are constantly seeking to improve the specification, design and production of their vehicles and alterations take place accordingly. While every effort has been made to ensure the accuracy of this Manual, it should not be regarded as an infallible guide to current specifications of any particular vehicle.

This Manual does not constitute an offer for sale of any particular component or vehicle. Land Rover dealers are not agents of the Company and have no authority to bind the manufacturer by any expressed or implied undertaking or representation.

DATA

Firing order 1, 8, 4, 3, 6, 5, 7, 2
Cylinders 1, 3, 5, 7 - LH side of engine
Cylinders 2, 4, 6, 8 - RH side of engine

Cylinder heads
Maximum warp	0.05 mm	0.002 in
Reface limit	0.50 mm	0.02 in

Valve springs
Free length	48.30 mm	1.90 in
Fitted length	40.40 mm	1.60 in
Load - valve open	736 ± 10 N	165 ± 2 lbf
Load - valve closed	339 ± 10 N	76 ± 2 lbf

Valves
Valve stem diameter:
Inlet	8.664 to 8.679 mm	0.341 to 0.342 in
Exhaust	8.651 to 8.666 mm	0.340 to 0.341 in

Valve head diameter:
Inlet	39.75 to 40.00 mm	1.5 to 1.6 in
Exhaust	34.226 to 34.480 mm	1.3 to 1.4 in
Valve installed height - maximum	47.63 mm	1.9 in

Valve stem to guide clearance:
Inlet	0.025 to 0.066 mm	0.001 to 0.002 in
Exhaust	0.038 to 0.078 mm	0.0015 to 0.003 in

Valve guides
Valve guide installed height	15.0 mm	0.590 in
Inside diameter after reaming	8.7 mm	0.34 in

Valve seats
Valve seat angle	46° to 46° 25'	

Valve seat width:
Inlet	36.83 mm	1.45 in
Exhaust	31.50 mm	1.24 in

Valve seating width:
Inlet	0.89 to 1.4 mm	0.035 to 0.055 in
Exhaust	1.32 to 1.83 mm	0.052 to 0.072 in
Valve seating face angle	45°	

Oil pump
Inner to outer rotor clearance - maximum	0.25 mm	0.01 in
Rotors to cover plate clearance - maximum	0.1 mm	0.004 in
Drive gear wear step depth - maximum	0.15 mm	0.006 in

Oil pressure relief valve
Spring free length	60.0 mm	2.4 in

Camshaft
End-float	0.05 to 0.35 mm	0.002 to 0.014 in
Maximum run-out	0.05 mm	0.002 in

Piston rings
Ring to groove clearance:

1st compression	0.05 to 0.10 mm	0.002 to 0.004 in
2nd compression	0.05 to 0.10 mm	0.002 to 0.004 in

Ring fitted gap:

1st compression	0.3 to 0.5 mm	0.01 to 0.02 in
2nd compression	0.40 to 0.65 mm	0.016 to 0.03 in
Oil control rails	0.38 to 1.40 mm	0.014 to 0.05 in
Oil control ring width	3.00 mm	0.12 in - maximum

Pistons
Piston diameter:

Production - Grade A	93.970 to 93.985 mm	3.700 to 3.7002 in
Production - Grade B*	93.986 to 94.0 mm	3.7003 to 3.701 in
Clearance in bore	0.02 to 0.045 mm	0.001 to 0.002 in

Gudgeon pins

Length	60.00 to 60.50 mm	2.35 to 2.4 in
Diameter	23.995 to 24.000 mm	0.94 to 0.95 in
Clearance in piston	0.006 to 0.015 mm	0.0002 to 0.0006 in

Connecting rods
Length between centres:

4.0 litre	155.12 to 155.22 mm	6.10 to 6.11 in
4.6 litre	149.68 to 149.78 mm	5.89 to 5.91 in

Cylinder bore
Cylinder bore:

Grade A piston fitted	94.00 to 94.015 mm	3.700 to 3.701 in
Grade B piston fitted	94.016 to 94.030 mm	3.7014 to 3.702 in
Cylinder bore maximum ovality	0.013 mm	0.0005 in

Crankshaft

Main journal diameter	63.487 to 63.500 mm	2.499 to 2.52 in
Minimum regrind diameter	62.979 to 62.992 mm	2.509 to 2.510 in
Maximum out of round	0.040 mm	0.002 in
Big-end journal diameter	55.500 to 55.513 mm	2.20 to 2.22 in
Minimum regrind diameter	54.992 to 55.005 mm	2.16 to 2.165 in
Maximum out of round	0.040 mm	0.002 in
End-float	0.10 to 0.20 mm	0.004 to 0.008 in
Maximum run-out	0.08 mm	0.003 in

Main bearings

Main bearing diametrical clearance	0.010 to 0.048 mm	0.0004 to 0.002 in
Oversizes	0.254, 0.508 mm	0.01, 0.02 in

Big-end bearings

Big-end bearing diametrical clearance	0.015 to 0.055 mm	0.0006 to 0.0021 in
Oversizes	0.254, 0.508 mm	0.01, 0.02 in
End-float on journal	0.15 to 0.36 mm	0.006 to 0.01 in

Flywheel

Flywheel minimum thickness	40.45 mm	1.6 in

Drive plate
Drive plate setting height:

Up to engine no. 42D00593A - 4.0 litre	21.25 to 21.37 mm	0.83 to 0.84 in
Up to engine no. 46D00450A - 4.6 litre	7.69 to 7.81 mm	0.30 to 0.31 in

* Grade B piston supplied as service replacement

ENGINE

Crankshaft pulley bolt	270 Nm	200 lbf.ft
Camshaft gear bolt	50 Nm	37 lbf.ft
Camshaft thrust plate bolts	25 Nm	18 lbf.ft
Rocker cover bolts: +		
Stage 1	4 Nm	3 lbf.ft
Stage 2	8 Nm	6 lbf.ft
Stage 3 - re-torque to:	8 Nm	6 lbf.ft
Rocker shaft to cylinder head bolts	38 Nm	28 lbf.ft
Cylinder head bolts: +*		
Stage 1	20 Nm	15 lbf.ft
Stage 2	Then 90 degrees	
Stage 3	Further 90 degrees	
Lifting eye to cylinder head bolts	40 Nm	30 lbf.ft
Connecting rod bolts:		
Stage 1	20 Nm	15 lbf.ft
Stage 2	Further 80 degrees	
Main bearing cap bolts - Nos. 1 to 8: +		
Stage 1 - initial torque	13.5 Nm	10 lbf.ft
Stage 2 - final torque	72 Nm	53 lbf.ft
Rear main bearing cap bolts - Nos. 9 and 10: +		
Stage 1 - initial torque	13.5 Nm	10 lbf.ft
Stage 2 - final torque	92 Nm	68 lbf.ft
Main bearing cap side bolts - Nos. 11 to 20: +		
Stage 1 - initial torque	13.5 Nm	10 lbf.ft
Stage 2 - final torque	45 Nm	33 lbf.ft
Flywheel bolts	80 Nm	59 lbf.ft
Drive plate assembly bolts	45 Nm	33 lbf.ft
Drive plate hub aligner to crankshaft socket head cap screws	85 Nm	63 lbf.ft
Oil sump drain plug	45 Nm	33 lbf.ft
Oil sump nuts and bolts + ...	23 Nm	17 lbf.ft
Oil pump cover plate screws **	4 Nm	3 lbf.ft
Oil pump cover plate bolt **	8 Nm	6 lbf.ft
Spark plugs	20 Nm	15 lbf.ft
Timing cover/coolant pump to cylinder block bolts + ...	22 Nm	16 lbf.ft
Oil pick-up pipe to oil pump bolts	8 Nm	6 lbf.ft
Oil pick-up pipe nut	24 Nm	18 lbf.ft
Knock sensors to cylinder block	16 Nm	12 lbf.ft
Camshaft sensor to timing cover bolt	8 Nm	6 lbf.ft
Crankshaft position sensor bolts	6 Nm	4 lbf.ft
Oil cooler connections	15 Nm	11 lbf.ft

+ Tighten in sequence
* Lightly oil threads prior to assembly.
** Coat threads with Loctite 222 prior to assembly.

INFORMATION

GENERAL

For bolts and nuts not otherwise specified

M5	4 Nm	3 lbf.ft
M6	6 Nm	4 lbf.ft
M8	18 Nm	13 lbf.ft
M10	35 Nm	26 lbf.ft
M12	65 Nm	48 lbf.ft
M14	80 Nm	59 lbf.ft
M16	130 Nm	96 lbf.ft
1/4 UNC/UNF	9 Nm	7 lbf.ft
5/16 UNC and UNF	25 Nm	18 lbf.ft
3/8 UNC and UNF	40 Nm	30 lbf.ft
7/16 UNC and UNF	75 Nm	55 lbf.ft
1/2 UNC and UNF	90 Nm	66 lbf.ft
5/8 UNC and UNF	135 Nm	100 lbf.ft

SERVICE TOOLS

Land Rover Number	Rover Number	Description
LRT-12-013	18G1150	Remover/replacer - gudgeon pin
LRT-12-126/1	-	Adapter - remover/replacer - gudgeon pin
LRT-12-126/2	-	Adapter - remover/replacer - gudgeon pin
LRT-12-126/3	-	Parallel sleeve - gudgeon pin
LRT-12-034	18G1519A	Valve spring compressor
LRT-12-037	RO274401	Drift - remover - valve guide
LRT-12-038	RO600959	Drift - replacer - valve guide
LRT-12-055	-	Distance piece - valve guide
LRT-12-089	-	Replacer - timing cover oil seal
LRT-12-090	-	Retainer - oil pump gears
LRT-12-091	-	Replacer - crankshaft rear oil seal
LRT-12-095	-	Protection sleeve - crankshaft rear oil seal
LRT-12-501	MS76B	Basic handle set - valve seat cutters
LRT-12-503	MS150-8.5	Adjustable valve seat pilot
LRT-12-515	RO605774A	Distance piece - valve guide
LRT-12-517	-	Adjustable valve seat cutter

Service tools must be obtained direct from the manufacturers:
V.L. Churchill,
P.O. Box No 3,
London Road,
Daventry,
Northants, NN11 4NF
England.

CONTENTS

CONTENTS

Page

This page is intentionally left blank

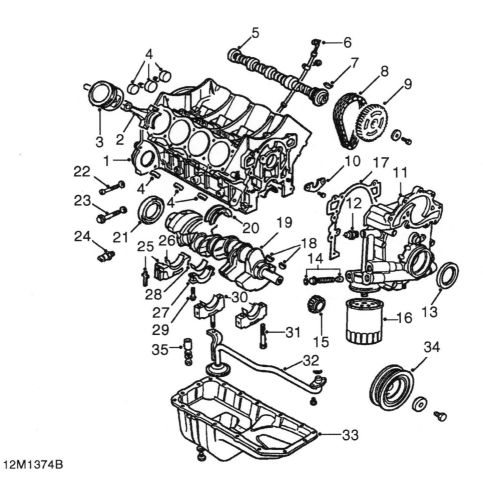

12M1374B

CYLINDER BLOCK COMPONENTS

1. Cylinder block
2. Connecting rod
3. Piston and gudgeon pin
4. Core plugs
5. Camshaft
6. Dipstick
7. Camshaft Woodruff key
8. Timing chain
9. Camshaft sprocket
10. Thrust plate
11. Timing cover and oil pump assembly *
12. Oil pressure switch
13. Timing cover oil seal
14. Oil pressure relief valve assembly
15. Crankshaft sprocket
16. Oil filter
17. Timing cover gasket
18. Woodruff keys

19. Crankshaft
20. Centre main bearing shell - upper
21. Crankshaft rear oil seal
22. Main bearing socket head cap bolt
23. Main bearing hexagonal head bolt
24. Crankshaft knock sensor
25. Rear main bearing cap and side seals
26. Rear main bearing shell
27. Big end bearing cap
28. Big end bearing shell
29. Big end bearing bolt
30. Centre and front main bearing caps
31. Main bearing cap bolt
32. Oil pick-up pipe
33. Sump
34. Crankshaft pulley
35. Oil pick-up pipe spacer, washers and nut

* New Range Rover timing
   cover illustrated

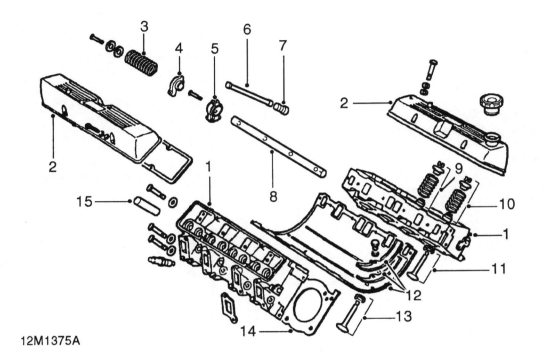

12M1375A

CYLINDER HEAD COMPONENTS

1. Cylinder head
2. Rocker cover
3. Rocker shaft spring
4. Rocker arm
5. Rocker shaft bracket
6. Pushrod
7. Tappet
8. Rocker shaft
9. Inlet valve seal, spring, cap and collets
10. Exhaust valve seal, spring, cap and collets
11. Exhaust valve and seat
12. Inlet manifold gasket and seals
13. Inlet valve and seat
14. Cylinder head gasket
15. Valve guide

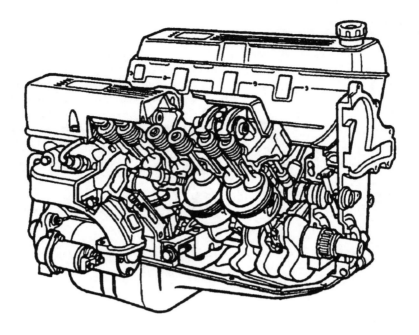

12M1384

OPERATION

The V8 engine is an eight cylinder, water cooled unit comprising cast aluminium cylinder block and cylinder heads.

The cast iron cylinder liners are shrink fitted and located on stops in the cylinder block. The banks of cylinders are at 90° to each other. The crankshaft is carried in five main bearings, end-float being controlled by the thrust faces of the upper centre main bearing shell.

The centrally located camshaft is driven by the crankshaft via a chain. The valves are operated by rockers, pushrods and hydraulic tappets. Exhaust valves used on later engines are of the 'carbon break' type which incorporate a machined undercut at the combustion chamber end of the valve. The design prevents carbon build-up on the valve stem which could lead to valves sticking. These valves are interchangeable with valves fitted to early engines.

Each of the aluminium alloy pistons has two compression rings and an oil control ring. The pistons are secured to the connecting rods by semi-floating gudgeon pins. The gudgeon pin is offset 0.5 mm (0.02 in), identified by an arrow mark on the piston crown, which must always point to the front of the engine. Plain, big-end bearing shells are fitted to each connecting rod.

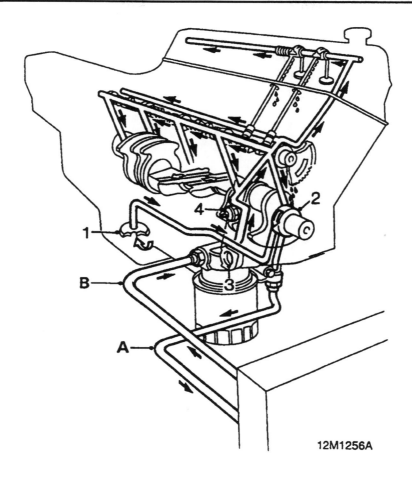

12M1256A

1. Oil strainer
2. Oil pump
3. Pressure relief valve

4. Oil pressure switch
   A Oil to cooler
   B Oil from cooler

Lubrication

The full flow lubrication system uses a gear type oil pump driven from the crankshaft. The assembly is integral with the timing cover which also carries the full flow oil filter, oil pressure switch and pressure relief valve.

Oil is drawn from the pressed steel sump through a strainer and into the oil pump, excess pressure being relieved by the pressure relief valve. The oil pressure warning light switch is screwed into the timing cover and registers the oil pressure in the main oil gallery on the outflow side of the filter.

Pressurised oil passes through an oil cooler mounted in front of the radiator to the full flow oil filter. The oil then passes through internal drillings to the crankshaft where it is directed to each main bearing and to the big end bearings via numbers 1, 3 and 5 main bearings.

An internal drilling in the cylinder block directs oil to the camshaft where it passes through further internal drillings to the hydraulic tappets, camshaft journals and rocker shaft. Lubrication to the thrust side of the cylinders is either by oil grooves machined in each connecting rod big end joint face or by splash.

Hydraulic tappets

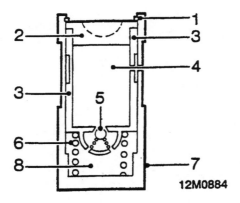

12M0884

1. Clip
2. Pushrod seat
3. Inner sleeve
4. Upper chamber
5. Non-return ball valve
6. Spring
7. Outer sleeve
8. Lower chamber

The purpose of the hydraulic tappet is to provide maintenance free and quiet operation of valves. It achieves this by utilising engine oil pressure to eliminate the mechanical clearance between the rockers and the valve stems.

During normal operation, engine oil pressure, present in the upper chamber, passes through the non-return ball valve and into the lower chamber.

When the cam begins to lift the outer sleeve, the resistance of the valve spring, felt through the push rod and seat, causes the tappet inner sleeve to move downwards inside the outer sleeve. This downward movement of the inner sleeve closes the ball valve and increases the pressure in the lower chamber sufficiently to ensure that the push rod opens the valve fully.

As the tappet moves off the peak of the cam, the ball valve opens to equalise the pressure in both chambers which ensures the valve closes when the tappet is on the back of the cam.

ROCKER SHAFTS

Rocker shafts - remove

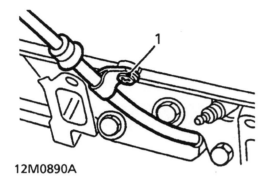

12M0890A

1. *LH rocker shaft only:* Remove screw securing dipstick tube to rocker cover.

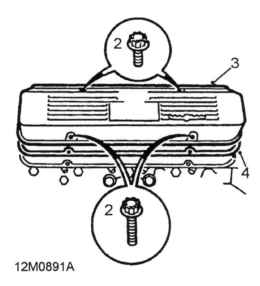

12M0891A

2. Remove 4 bolts securing rocker cover to cylinder head.

 NOTE: Mark position of 2 longer bolts.

3. Remove rocker cover.
4. Remove and discard gasket from rocker cover.

5. Mark each rocker shaft in relation to original cylinder head.

⚠ CAUTION: Incorrect fitment of rocker shafts will lead to an oil feed restriction.

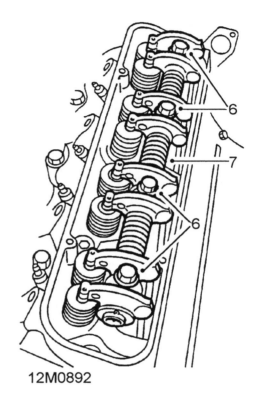

12M0892

6. Progressively slacken and remove 4 bolts securing rocker shaft assembly to cylinder head.
7. Remove rocker shaft assembly.
8. Remove pushrods and store in fitted order.

Rocker shafts - dismantling

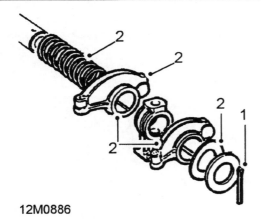

12M0886

1. Remove and discard split pin from one end of rocker shaft.
2. Remove plain washer, wave washer, rocker arms, brackets and springs.

Inspecting components

1. Thoroughly clean components.
2. Inspect each component for wear, in particular rocker arms and shafts. Discard weak or broken springs.
3. Inspect pushrod seats in rocker arms.
4. Check pushrods for straightness and inspect ball ends for damage, replace as necessary.

Rocker shafts - assembling

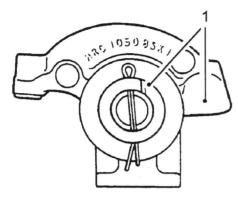

12M0887

1. Assemble rocker shafts with identification groove at one o'clock position with push rod end of rocker arm to the right.

 CAUTION: Incorrect assembly of rocker shafts will lead to an oil feed restriction.

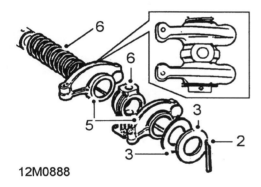

12M0888

2. Fit new split pin to one end of rocker shaft.
3. Fit plain washer and wave washer.
4. Lubricate rocker arm bushes with engine oil.
5. Fit rocker arms with offsets as illustrated.
6. Assemble rocker arms, brackets and springs to rocker shaft.
7. Compress springs, fit wave washer, plain washer and secure with new split pin.

Rocker shafts - refit

1. Lubricate pushrods with engine oil.
2. Fit pushrods in removed order.

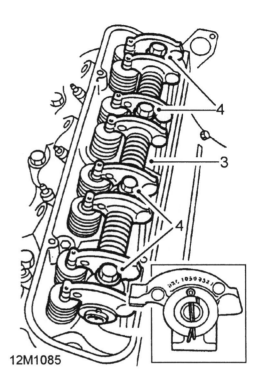

12M1085

3. Fit each rocker shaft assembly, ensuring identification groove is uppermost and towards front of engine on RH side and towards rear of engine on LH side.

CAUTION: Incorrect fitment of rocker shafts will lead to an oil feed restriction.

4. Fit bolts and starting at centre brackets, tighten to 38 Nm (28 lbf.ft).

5. Clean gasket surface in rocker cover.

 NOTE: Gaskets fitted to early engines were manufactured from cork whilst those fitted to later engines are manufactured from rubber. The later type gaskets should be fitted as replacements to all engines. Cork gaskets were retained by an adhesive whereas rubber gaskets do not need an adhesive. If cork gaskets were originally fitted, remove all traces of adhesive using Bostik Cleaner 6001 or equivalent.

6. Fit new gasket, dry to rocker cover.
7. Fit rocker cover to cylinder head, fit bolts and tighten in diagonal sequence to:
   Stage 1 - 4 Nm (3 lbf.ft)
   Stage 2 - 8 Nm (6 lbf.ft)
   Stage 3 - Re-torque to 8 Nm (6 lbf.ft)

⚠ **CAUTION: The 2 short bolts must be fitted on side of cover nearest centre of engine.**

8. *LH rocker shaft only:* Align dipstick tube to rocker cover, fit and tighten screw.

CYLINDER HEAD

Cylinder head - remove

1. Remove rocker shaft assembly.
2. Mark heads LH and RH for reassembly.

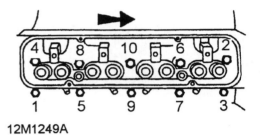

12M1249A

⚠ NOTE: RH cylinder head illustrated.

3. Using sequence shown, remove and discard 10 bolts securing cylinder head to cylinder block.
4. Release cylinder head from 2 dowels and remove cylinder head.
5. Remove and discard cylinder head gasket.
6. Repeat above procedures for remaining cylinder head.

Valves and springs - remove

1. Remove spark plugs.

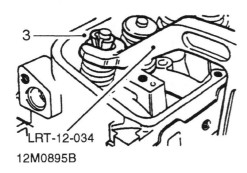

LRT-12-034

12M0895B

2. Using valve spring compressor **LRT-12-034** or a suitable alternative, compress valve spring.
3. Compress valve spring sufficiently to release collets from valve spring cap.

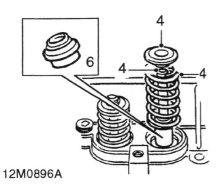

12M0896A

4. Release spring compressor and remove collets, valve, valve spring cap and valve spring.
5. Repeat above operations for remaining valves.

 NOTE: Keep valves, springs, caps and collets in fitted order.

6. Remove and discard valve stem oil seals.

Cylinder head - inspection

1. Clean all traces of gasket material from cylinder head using a plastic scraper.
2. Check core plugs for signs of leakage and corrosion, replace as necessary. Apply Loctite 572 to threads of screwed core plugs.

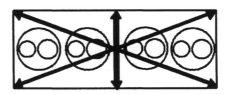

12M2902A

3. Check gasket face of each cylinder head for warping, across centre and from corner to corner.
Maximum warp = 0.05 mm (0.002 in)

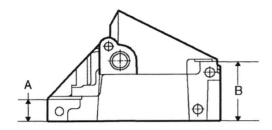

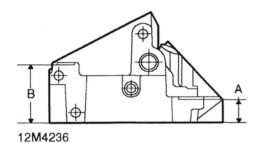

12M4236

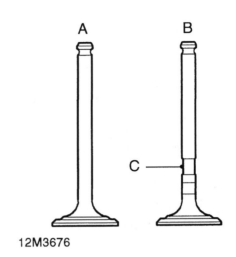

12M3676

4. Check cylinder head height at each end of
   cylinder head:
   A= 22.94 mm (0.903 in) - New
   B= 62.56 mm (2.463 in) - New

5. Cylinder heads may be refaced:
   Reface limit = 0.50 mm (0.02 in) from new
   dimension

⚠ NOTE: Two types of exhaust valve may be
fitted - standard valves A in illustration or
carbon break valves - B in illustration.
Carbon break valves may be identified by the
machined profile C on the valve stem. To prevent
exhaust valves sticking, standard exhaust valves
should be replaced with carbon break valves
during engine overhaul.

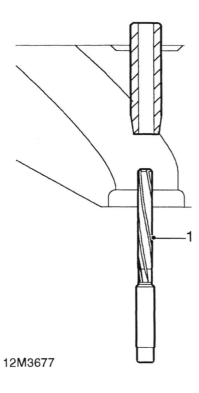

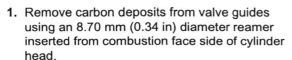

12M3677

1. Remove carbon deposits from valve guides using an 8.70 mm (0.34 in) diameter reamer inserted from combustion face side of cylinder head.
2. Clean valve springs, cotters, caps and valves. Clean inlet valve guide bores. Ensure all loose particles of carbon are removed on completion.
3. Check existing valve stem and head diameters.
4. Check valve stem to guide clearance using new valves.

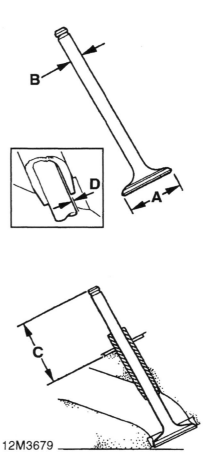

12M3679

5. Renew valves and guides as necessary. Valve head diameter **A**:
   Inlet = 39.75 to 40.00 mm (1.5 to 1.6 in)
   Exhaust = 34.226 to 34.48 mm (1.3 to 1.4 in)
   Valve stem diameter **B**:
   Inlet = 8.664 to 8.679 mm (0.341 to 0.342 in)
   Exhaust = 8.651 to 8.666 mm (0.340 to 0.341 in)
6. Check installed height of each valve.
   Valve installed height **C** = 47.63 mm (1.9 in)
7. Renew valve/valve seat insert as necessary.
8. Check valve stem to guide clearance.
   Valve stem to guide clearance **D**:
   Inlet = 0.025 to 0.066 mm (0.001 to 0.002 in)
   Exhaust = 0.038 to 0.078 mm (0.0015 to 0.003 in)

9. Check condition of valve springs:
   Free length = 48.30 mm (1.90 in)
   Fitted length = 40.40 mm (1.60 in)
   Load - valve closed = 339 ± 10 N (76 ± 2 lbf)
   Load - valve open = 736 ± 10 N (165 ± 2 lbf)

 NOTE: Valve springs must be replaced as a complete set.

Valve guides - renew

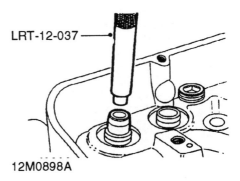

LRT-12-037

12M0898A

1. Using valve guide remover, **LRT-12-037** press valve guide out into combustion face side of cylinder head.

 NOTE: Service valve guides are 0.025 mm (0.001 in) oversize on outside diameter to ensure interference fit.

2. Lubricate new valve guide with engine oil and place in position.

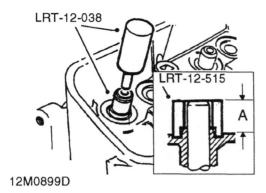

LRT-12-038

LRT-12-515

A

12M0899D

Valve seat inserts - inspection

1. Check valve seat inserts for pitting, burning and wear. Replace inserts as necessary.

3. Using **LRT-12-038** partially press guide into cylinder head, remove tool.
4. Fit **LRT-12-515** over valve guide and continue to press guide into cylinder head until tool **LRT-12-038** contacts tool **LRT-12-515**; remove tool.
   Valve guide installed height **A** = 15.0 mm (0.590 in)
5. Ream valve guides to 8.70 mm (0.34 in) diameter.
6. Remove all traces of swarf on completion.

Valve seat inserts - renew

 NOTE: Service valve seat inserts are available 0.025 mm (0.001 in) oversize on outside diameter to ensure interference fit.

1. Remove worn valve seats.

 CAUTION: Take care not to damage counterbore in cylinder head.

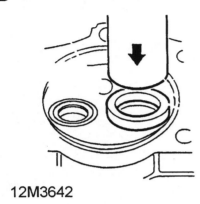

12M3642

2. Heat cylinder head evenly to approximately 120° C (250° F).

 WARNING: Handle hot cylinder head with care.

3. Using a suitable mandrel, press new insert fully into counterbore.
4. Allow cylinder head to air cool.

Valve seats and seat inserts - refacing

 CAUTION: Renew worn valve guides and seat inserts before lapping valves to their seats.

1. Check condition of valve seats and valves that are to be re-used.
2. Remove carbon from valve seats.

12M0901

3. Reface valves as necessary. If a valve has to be ground to a knife-edge to obtain a true seat, fit a new valve.
Valve seating face angle **A** = 45°

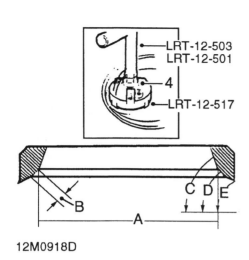

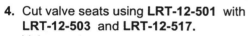

12M0918D

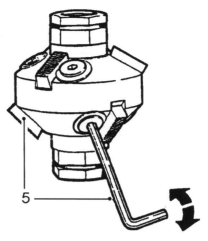

12M0902

4. Cut valve seats using **LRT-12-501** with
   LRT-12-503 and **LRT-12-517.**
   Valve seat:
   Width **A:**
   Inlet = 36.83 mm (1.45 in)
   Exhaust = 31.50 mm (1.24 in)

   Seating width **B:**
   Inlet = 0.89 to 1.4 mm (0.035 to 0.055 in)
   Exhaust = 1.32 to 1.83 mm (0.052 to 0.072 in)

   Angle **C**= 56° to 70°
   Angle **D**= 46° to 46° 25'
   Angle **E**= 20°

5. Ensure cutter blades are correctly fitted to
   cutter head with angled end of blade
   downwards, facing work, as illustrated. Check
   that cutter blades are adjusted so that middle
   of blade contacts area of material to be cut.
   Use light pressure and remove only minimum
   of material necessary.
6. Remove all traces of swarf on completion.

Valves - lapping-in

1. Lap each valve to its seat using fine grinding paste.
2. Clean valve and seat.

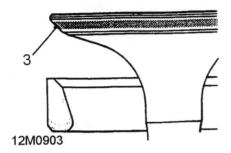

12M0903

3. Coat valve seat with a small quantity of engineer's blue, insert valve and press it into position several times without rotating. Remove valve and check for even and central seating. Seating position shown by engineer's blue should be in centre of valve face.

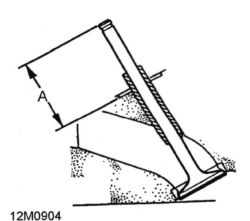

12M0904

4. Check valve installed height if valve seats have been recut or new valves or valve seat inserts have been fitted.
   Valve installed height A= 47.63 mm (1.9 in) - maximum
5. Thoroughly clean cylinder head, blow out oilways and coolant passages.

Valves and springs - refit

1. Fit new valve stem oil seals, lubricate valve stems, fit valves, valve springs and caps, compress valve springs using **LRT-12-034** and fit collets.
2. Using a wooden dowel and mallet, lightly tap each valve stem two or three times to seat valve cap and collets.
3. Fit spark plugs and tighten to 20 Nm (15 lbf.ft).

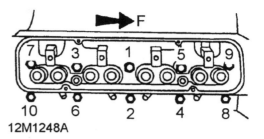

Cylinder head - refit

1. Clean cylinder block and cylinder head faces using suitable gasket removal spray and a plastic scraper.
2. Eensure that bolt holes in cylinder block are clean and dry.

 CAUTION: Do not use metal scraper or machined surfaces may be damaged.

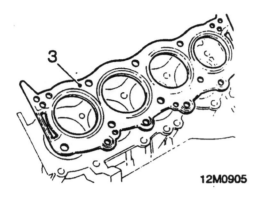

12M0905

3. Fit cylinder head gasket with the word 'TOP' uppermost.

 NOTE: Gasket must be fitted dry.

4. Carefully fit cylinder head and locate on dowels.

5. Lightly oil threads of new cylinder head bolts.

12M1248A

 NOTE: RH cylinder head illustrated.

6. Fit new cylinder head bolts:
   Long bolts: 1, 3 and 5
   Short bolts: 2, 4, 6, 7, 8, 9 and 10
7. Using sequence shown, tighten cylinder head bolts to:
   Stage 1 - 20 Nm (15 lbf.ft)
   Stage 2 - 90 degrees
   Stage 3 - Further 90 degrees

 CAUTION: Do not tighten bolts 180° in one operation.

8. Fit rocker shaft assembly.
9. Repeat above procedures for remaining cylinder head.

TIMING CHAIN AND GEARS

Sump - remove

1. Remove dipstick.

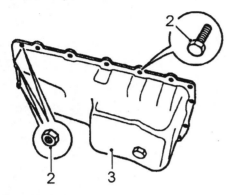

12M1377A

2. Remove 14 bolts and 3 nuts securing sump to cylinder block and timing cover.
3. Taking care not to damage sealing faces, carefully release sump from timing cover and cylinder block.
4. Remove sump.

Timing cover - remove

⚠️ NOTE: Timing cover, oil pump and oil pressure relief valve are only supplied as an assembly.

1. Using assistance, restrain flywheel/drive plate and remove crankshaft pulley bolt; collect spacer washer - if fitted.
2. Remove crankshaft pulley.
3. Remove sump.

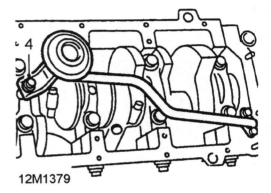

12M1379

4. Remove nut and washers securing oil pick-up pipe to stud.

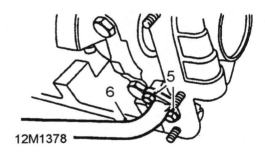

12M1378

5. Remove 2 bolts securing oil pick-up pipe to oil pump cover, withdraw pipe from cover; remove and discard 'O' ring.
6. Remove oil pick-up pipe, recover spacer from stud.

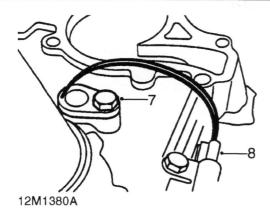

12M1380A

7. Remove bolt securing camshaft sensor to timing cover, withdraw sensor; remove and discard 'O' ring.
8. Release harness connector from mounting bracket.

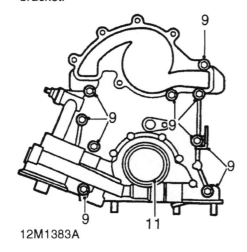

12M1383A

 NOTE: New Range Rover timing cover illustrated.

9. Noting their fitted position, remove 9 bolts securing timing cover to cylinder block; remove cover; collect camshaft sensor harness mounting bracket.

 NOTE: Timing cover is dowel located.

 CAUTION: Do not attempt to remove oil pump drive gear at this stage.

10. Remove and discard gasket.
11. Remove and discard oil seal from timing cover.

Timing gears - remove

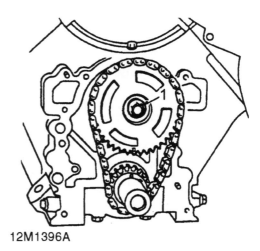

12M1396A

1. Restrain camshaft gear and remove bolt securing gear.

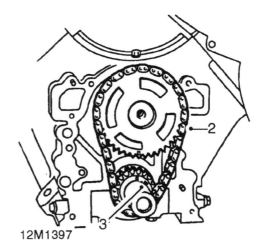

12M1397

2. Remove timing chain and gears as an assembly.
3. Collect Woodruff key from crankshaft.

Timing chain and gears - inspection

1. Thoroughly clean all components.
2. Inspect timing chain links and pins for wear.
3. Inspect timing chain gears for wear. Replace components as necessary.

Timing gears - refit

1. Clean gear locations on camshaft and crankshaft, fit Woodruff key to crankshaft.

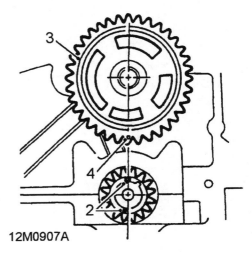

12M0907A

2. Temporarily fit crankshaft gear and if necessary, turn crankshaft to bring timing mark on gear to the twelve o'clock position, remove gear.
3. Temporarily fit camshaft gear.
4. Turn camshaft until mark on camshaft sprocket is at the six o'clock position, remove gear without moving camshaft.

Timing cover - refit

12M0914A

NOTE: Timing cover, oil pump and oil pressure relief valve are only supplied as an assembly.

1. Clean sealant from threads of timing cover bolts.
2. Clean all traces of gasket material from mating faces of timing cover and cylinder block.

CAUTION: Use a plastic scraper.

3. Clean oil seal location in timing cover.
4. Lubricate oil pump gears and oil seal recesses in timing cover with engine oil.
5. Apply Hylosil jointing compound to new timing cover gasket, position gasket to cylinder block.

5. Position timing gears on work surface with timing marks aligned.
6. Fit timing chain around gears, keeping timing marks aligned.
7. Fit gear and chain assembly.

NOTE: Timing marks must be facing forwards.

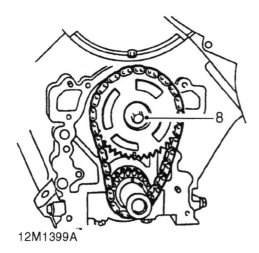

12M1399A

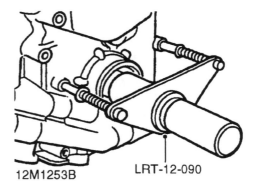

12M1253B   LRT-12-090

6. Locate tool **LRT-12-090** on timing cover and oil pump drive gear.
7. Position timing cover to cylinder block and at the same time, rotate tool **LRT-12-090** until drive gear keyway is aligned with Woodruff key.
8. Fit timing cover to cylinder block.

8. Fit camshaft gear bolt, restrain camshaft gear and tighten bolt to 50 Nm (37 lbf.ft).

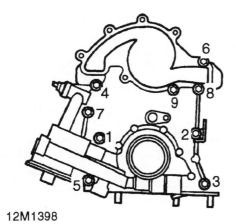

12M1398

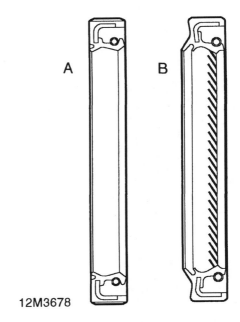

12M3678

NOTE: New Range Rover timing cover illustrated.

9. Position camshaft sensor harness mounting bracket to timing cover ensuring that bracket is positioned parallel to crankshaft centre line. Fit bolts and tighten in sequence shown to 22 Nm (16 lbf.ft).

CAUTION: Do not fit coolant pump bolts at this stage.

10. Remove tool **LRT-12-090**.

A- Early type seal
B- Later type seal - use as replacement on all engines

11. Lubricate new timing cover oil seal with Shell Retinax LX grease ensuring that space between seal lips is filled with grease.

CAUTION: Do not use any other type of grease.

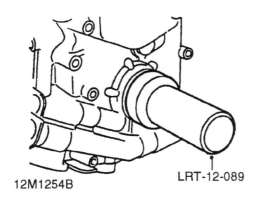

12M1254B   LRT-12-089

12. Fit timing cover oil seal using tool **LRT-12-089**.
13. Smear a new 'O' ring with engine oil and fit to oil pick-up pipe.
14. Position oil pick-up pipe spacer on number 4 main bearing cap stud.
15. Fit oil pick-up pipe ensuring that end of pipe is correctly inserted in oil pump body.
16. Fit oil pick-up pipe to oil pump body bolts and tighten to 8 Nm (6 lbf.ft).
17. Fit washers and nut securing oil pick-up pipe to stud, tighten nut to 24 Nm (18 lbf.ft).
18. Smear a new 'O' ring with engine oil and fit to camshaft sensor.
19. Insert camshaft sensor into timing cover, fit bolt and tighten to 8 Nm (6 lbf.ft).
20. Position camshaft sensor harness connector on mounting bracket.
21. Fit sump.
22. Fit crankshaft pulley, fit bolt and spacer washer - if fitted; tighten bolt to 270 Nm (200 lbf.ft).

 NOTE: Crankshaft pulleys which incorporate a mud flinger can be fitted to all engines.

Sump - refit

1. Remove all traces of old sealant from mating faces of cylinder block and sump.

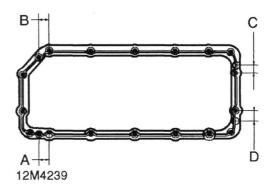

12M4239

2. Clean mating faces with suitable solvent and apply a bead of Hylosil Type 101 or 106 sealant to sump joint face as shown:
   Bead width - areas A, B, C and D = 12 mm (0.5 in)
   Bead width - remaining areas = 5 mm (0.20 in)
   Bead length - areas A and B = 32 mm (1.23 in)
   Bead length - areas C and D = 19 mm (0.75 in)

⚠ **CAUTION: Do not spread sealant bead. Sump must be fitted immediately after applying sealant.**

3. Fit sump, taking care not to damage sealant bead.

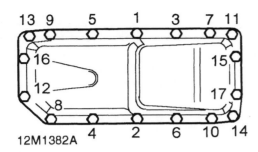

12M1382A

4. Fit sump bolts and nuts and working in sequence shown, tighten to 23 Nm (17 lbf.ft).
5. Fit sump drain plug and tighten to 45 Nm (33 lbf.ft).
6. Fit dipstick.

OIL PUMP AND OIL PRESSURE RELIEF VALVE

 NOTE: Overhaul procedures for the oil pump and oil pressure relief valve are limited to carrying out dimensional checks. In the event of wear or damage being found, a replacement timing cover and oil pump assembly must be fitted.

Oil pump - remove

1. Remove timing cover.

⚠ CAUTION: Do not attempt to remove oil pump drive gear from inner rotor at this stage.

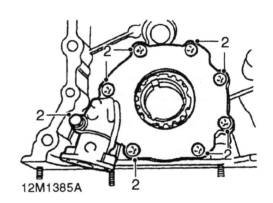

12M1385A

2. Remove 7 screws and bolt securing oil pump cover plate, remove plate.

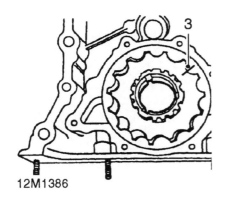

12M1386

3. Make suitable alignment marks on inner and outer rotors, remove rotors and oil pump drive gear as an assembly.

Oil pressure relief valve - remove

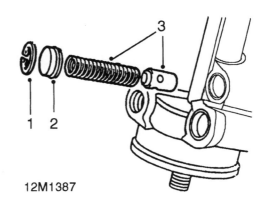

12M1387

1. Remove circlip.
2. Remove relief valve plug, remove and discard 'O' ring.
3. Remove relief valve spring and piston.

Oil pump - inspection

1. Thoroughly clean oil pump drive gear, cover plate, rotors and housing. Remove all traces of Loctite from cover plate securing screws; ensure tapped holes in timing cover are clean and free from oil.
2. Check mating surfaces of cover plate, rotors and housing for scoring.
3. Assemble rotors and oil pump drive gear in housing ensuring that reference marks are aligned.

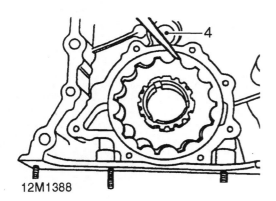

12M1388

4. Using feeler gauges, check clearance between teeth of inner and outer rotors:
   Maximum clearance = 0.25 mm (0.01 in)

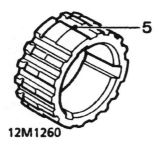

12M1260

5. Remove oil pump drive gear, check depth of any wear steps on gear teeth:
   Wear step maximum depth = 0.15 in (0.006 in)

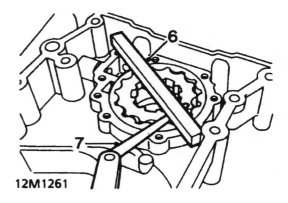

12M1261

6. Place a straight edge across housing.
7. Using feeler gauges, check clearance between straight edge and rotors:
   Maximum clearance = 0.1 mm (0.004 in).

Oil pressure relief valve - inspection

1. Clean relief valve components and piston bore in timing cover.
2. Check piston and bore for scoring and that piston slides freely in bore with no perceptible side movement.
3. Check relief valve spring for damage and distortion; check spring free length:
   Spring free length = 60.0 mm (2.4 in).

Oil pump - refit

1. Lubricate rotors, oil pump drive gear, cover plate and housing with engine oil.
2. Assemble rotors and drive gear in housing ensuring that reference marks are aligned.
3. Position cover plate to housing.
4. Apply Loctite 222 to threads of cover plate screws and bolt.
5. Fit cover plate screws and bolt and tighten to:-
   Screws - 4 Nm (3 lbf.ft)
   Bolt - 8 Nm (6 lbf.ft)
6. Fit timing cover.

Oil pressure relief valve - refit

1. Lubricate new 'O' ring with engine oil and fit to relief valve plug.
2. Lubricate relief valve spring, piston and piston bore with engine oil.
3. Assemble piston to relief valve spring, insert piston and spring into piston bore.
4. Fit relief valve plug, depress plug and fit circlip.
5. Ensure circlip is fully seated in groove.

CAMSHAFT AND TAPPETS

Camshaft end-float - check

1. Remove rocker shaft assemblies.
2. Remove pushrods and store in their fitted order.
3. Remove timing chain and gears.

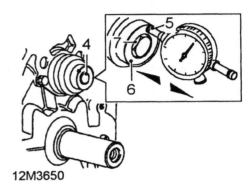

12M3650

4. Temporarily fit camshaft gear bolt.
5. Attach a suitable DTI to front of cylinder block with stylus of gauge contacting end of camshaft.
6. Push camshaft rearwards and zero gauge.
7. Using camshaft gear bolt, pull camshaft forwards and note end-float reading on gauge. End-float = 0.05 to 0.35 mm (0.002 to 0.014 in)

8. If end-float is incorrect, fit a new thrust plate and re-check. If end-float is still incorrect, a new camshaft must be fitted.

Camshaft and tappets - remove

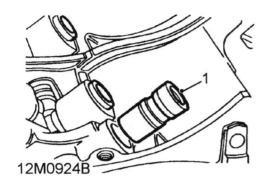

12M0924B

1. Remove tappets and retain with their respective pushrods.

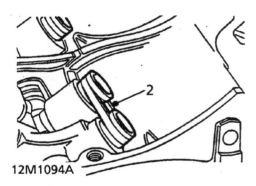

12M1094A

2. When tappets prove difficult to remove due to damaged camshaft contact area, proceed as follows. Lift tappets in pairs to the point where damaged face is about to enter tappet bore and fit rubber bands to retain tappets. Repeat until all tappets are retained clear of camshaft lobes. The tappets can then be withdrawn out the bottom of their bores when the sump and camshaft are removed.

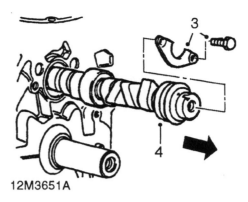

12M3651A

3. Remove 2 bolts securing camshaft thrust plate to cylinder block, remove plate.
4. Withdraw camshaft, taking care not to damage bearings in cylinder block.

⚠ NOTE: Camshafts fitted to 4.0 litre engines are colour coded ORANGE whilst those fitted to 4.6 litre engines are colour coded RED.

Camshaft and tappets - inspection

1. Thoroughly clean all components.
2. Inspect camshaft bearing journals and lobes for signs of wear, pitting, scoring and overheating.
3. Support camshaft front and rear bearings on vee blocks, and using a DTI, measure camshaft run-out on centre bearing: Maximum permitted run-out = 0.05 mm (0.002 in)
4. Inspect thrust plate for wear, replace plate if wear is evident.
5. Clean and inspect tappets. Check for an even, circular wear pattern on the camshaft contact area. If contact area is pitted or a square wear pattern has developed, tappet must be renewed.
6. Inspect tappet body for excessive wear or scoring. Replace tappet if scoring or deep wear patterns extend up to oil feed area. Clean and inspect tappet bores in cylinder block.
7. Ensure that tappets rotate freely in their respective bores.
8. Inspect pushrod contact area of tappet, replace tappet if surface is rough or pitted.

Camshaft and tappets - refit

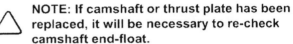 NOTE: If a replacement camshaft is to be fitted, ensure colour coding is correct. Camshafts fitted to 4.0 litre engines are colour coded ORANGE whilst those fitted to 4.6 litre engines are colour coded RED.

1. Lubricate camshaft journals with engine oil and carefully insert camshaft into cylinder block.
2. Fit camshaft thrust plate, fit bolts and tighten to 25 Nm (18 lbf.ft).

NOTE: If camshaft or thrust plate has been replaced, it will be necessary to re-check camshaft end-float.

3. Immerse tappets in engine oil. Before fitting, pump the inner sleeve of tappet several times using a pushrod to prime tappet; this will reduce tappet noise when engine is first started.
4. Lubricate tappet bores with engine oil and fit tappets in removed order.

NOTE: Some tappet noise may still be evident on initial start-up. If necessary, run the engine at 2500 rev/min for a few minutes until noise ceases.

5. Fit timing chain and gears.
6. Fit rocker shaft assemblies.

PISTONS, CONNECTING RODS, PISTON RINGS AND CYLINDER BORES

Pistons and connecting rods - remove

1. Remove cylinder head(s).
2. Remove big-end bearings.
3. Remove carbon ridge from top of each cylinder bore.
4. Suitably identify each piston to its respective cylinder bore.
5. Push connecting rod and piston assembly to top of cylinder bore and withdraw assembly.
6. Repeat above procedure for remaining pistons.

 CAUTION: Big-end bearing shells must be replaced whenever they are removed.

Piston rings - remove

1. Using a suitable piston ring expander, remove and discard piston rings.
2. Remove carbon from piston ring grooves.

 NOTE: Use an old broken piston ring with a squared-off end.

 CAUTION: Do not use a wire brush.

Piston rings - inspection

1. Temporarily fit new compression rings to piston.

 NOTE: If replacement pistons are to be fitted, ensure rings are correct for piston.

The 2nd compression ring marked 'TOP' must be fitted, with marking uppermost, into second groove. The 1st compression ring fits into top groove and can be fitted either way round.

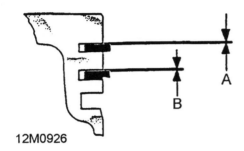

12M0926

2. Check compression ring to groove clearance:
   1st compression ring **A** = 0.05 to 0.10 mm (0.002 to 0.004 in).
   2nd compression ring **B** = 0.05 to 0.10 mm (0.002 to 0.004 in).

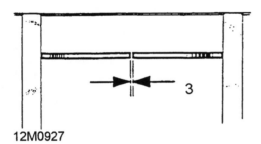

12M0927

3. Insert piston ring into its relevant cylinder bore, held square to bore with piston and check ring gaps.
   1st compression ring = 0.3 to 0.5 mm (0.01 to 0.02 in)
   2nd compression ring = 0.40 to 0.65 mm (0.016 to 0.03 in)
   Oil control ring rails = 0.38 to 1.40 mm (0.014 to 0.05 in)
4. Retain rings with their respective pistons.

Pistons- remove

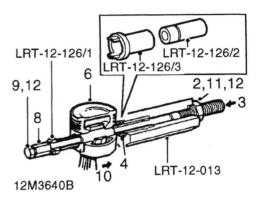

12M3640B

1. Clamp hexagon body of **LRT-12-013** in vice.
2. Screw large nut back until flush with end of centre screw.
3. Push centre screw forward until nut contacts thrust race.
4. Locate remover/replacer adapter **LRT-12-126/2** with its long spigot inside bore of hexagon body.
5. Position remover/replacer adapter **LRT-12-126/3** on **LRT-12-126/2** with cut-out facing away from body of **LRT-12-013**.
6. Locate piston and connecting rod assembly on centre screw and up to adapter **LRT-12-126/2.**
7. Position cut-out of adapter **LRT-12-126/3** to piston.

 CAUTION: Ensure cut-out does not contact gudgeon pin.

8. Fit remover/replacer bush **LRT-12-126/1** on centre screw with flanged end away from gudgeon pin. Screw stop nut on to centre screw.
9. Lock the stop nut securely with lockscrew.
10. Push connecting rod to right to locate end of gudgeon pin in adapter **LRT-12-126/2.**
11. Screw large nut up to **LRT-12-013** .
12. Hold lockscrew and turn large nut until gudgeon pin is withdrawn from piston.
13. Dismantle tool and remove piston, connecting rod and gudgeon pin.

 NOTE: Keep each piston and gudgeon pin with their respective connecting rod.

14. Repeat above operation for remaining pistons.

Pistons - inspection

1. Clean carbon from pistons.
2. Inspect pistons for distortion, cracks and burning.

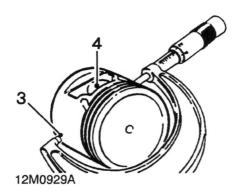

12M0929A

3. Measure and record piston diameter at 90° to gudgeon pin axis and 10 mm (0.4 in) from bottom of skirt.
4. Check gudgeon pin bore in piston for signs of wear and overheating.

 NOTE: Pistons fitted on production are graded 'A' or 'B,' the grade letter is stamped on the piston crown.

Production piston diameter:
Grade **A** = 93.970 to 93.985 mm (3.700 to 3.7002 in)
Grade **B** = 93.986 to 94.00 mm (3.7003 to 3.701 in)

Grade **B** pistons are supplied as service replacements. Worn cylinder liners fitted with grade 'A' pistons may be honed to accept grade 'B' pistons provided that specified cylinder bore and ovality limits are maintained.

⚠ CAUTION: Ensure replacement pistons are correct for the compression ratio of the engine. The compression ratio will be found on the cylinder block above the engine serial number. Ensure that replacement connecting rods are correct length for engine being overhauled.

Connecting rod length between centres:
4.0 litre = 155.12 to 155.22 mm (6.10 to 6.11 in)
4.6 litre = 149.68 to 149.78 mm (5.89 to 5.91 in)

Gudgeon pins - inspection

⚠ NOTE: Gudgeon pins are only supplied as an assembly with replacement pistons.

1. Check gudgeon pins for signs of wear and overheating.
2. Check clearance of gudgeon pin in piston. Gudgeon pin to piston clearance = 0.006 to 0.015 mm (0.0002 to 0.0006 in).
3. Check overall dimensions of gudgeon pin. Overall length = 60.00 to 60.50 mm (2.35 to 2.4 in).
Diameter - measured at each end and centre of pin = 23.995 to 24.00 mm (0.94 to 0.95 in).

Cylinder liner bore - inspection

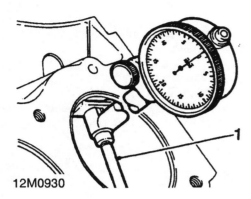

12M0930

2. If only new piston rings are to be fitted, break cylinder bore glazing using a fine grit, to produce a 60° cross-hatch finish. Ensure all traces of grit are removed after above operation.
3. Check alignment of connecting rods.

1. Measure cylinder liner bore wear and ovality in two axis 40 to 50 mm (1.5 to 1.9 in) from top of bore.
   Cylinder liner bore:
   Grade 'A' piston fitted = 94.00 to 94.015 mm (3.700 to 3.701 in)
   Grade 'B' piston fitted = 94.016 to 94.030 mm (3.7014 to 3.702 in)
   Maximum ovality = 0.013 mm (0.0005 in)
   Cylinder liners having grade 'A' pistons fitted may be honed to accept grade 'B' pistons provided specified wear and ovality limits are maintained.

 CAUTION: The temperature of piston and cylinder block must be the same to ensure accurate measurement.

Pistons - refit

⚠ **CAUTION: Pistons have a 0.5 mm (0.02 in) offset gudgeon pin which can be identified by an arrow mark on the piston crown. This arrow MUST always point to the front of the engine.**

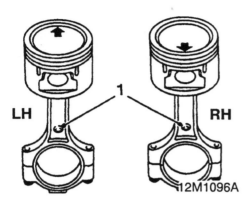

LH   RH

12M1096A

1. Assemble pistons to connecting rods with arrow on piston pointing towards domed shaped boss on connecting rod for RH bank of cylinders, and arrow pointing away from dome shaped boss for LH bank of cylinders.

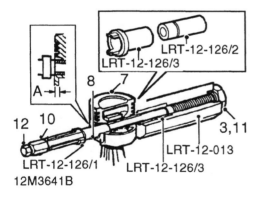

LRT-12-126/2
LRT-12-126/3
8 7
A
12 10
3,11
LRT-12-013
LRT-12-126/1
LRT-12-126/3
12M3641B

2. Clamp hexagon body of **LRT-12-013** in vice.
3. Slacken large nut and pull the centre screw 50.8 mm (2.0 in) out of hexagon body.
4. Locate remover/replacer adapter **LRT-12-126/2** with its long spigot inside bore of hexagon body.
5. Fit remover/replacer adapter **LRT-12-126/3** with cut-out towards piston, up to shoulder on centre screw.
6. Lubricate gudgeon pin and bores of connecting rod and piston with graphited oil.

7. Locate connecting rod and piston to centre screw with connecting rod entered on sleeve up to groove.
8. Fit gudgeon pin on to centre screw and into piston bore up to connecting rod.
9. Fit remover/replacer bush **LRT-12-126/1** with flanged end towards gudgeon pin.
10. Screw the stop nut onto centre screw and position piston against cut-out of adapter **LRT-12-126/3**.
11. Lubricate centre screw threads and thrust race with graphited oil, screw large nut up to **LRT-12-013**.
12. Lock the stop nut securely with lockscrew.
13. Set torque wrench to 16 Nm (12 lbf.ft), and using socket on large nut, pull gudgeon pin in until flange of **LRT-12-126/1** is distance **A** from face of piston.
Distance **A** = 0.4 mm (0.016 in).

⚠ **CAUTION: If torque wrench 'breaks' during above operation, fit of gudgeon pin to connecting rod is not acceptable and components must be replaced. The centre screw and thrust race must be kept well lubricated throughout operation.**

14. Dismantle tool, remove piston, check no damage has occurred during pressing and piston moves freely on gudgeon pin.
15. Repeat above operations for remaining pistons.

Piston to cylinder bore clearance - checking

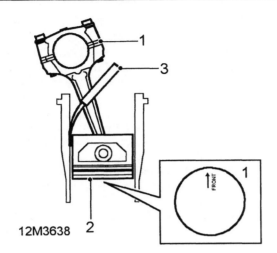

12M3638

1. Starting with number 1 piston, invert piston and with arrow on piston crown pointing towards REAR of cylinder block, insert piston in cylinder liner.
2. Position piston with bottom of skirt 30 mm (1.2 in) from top of cylinder block.
3. Using feeler gauges, measure and record clearance between piston and left hand side of cylinder - viewed from front of cylinder block: Piston to bore clearance = 0.02 to 0.045 mm (0.001 to 0.002 in)
4. Repeat above procedures for remaining pistons.

Pistons and connecting rods - refit

1. Fit oil control ring rails and expander, ensuring ends butt and do not overlap.

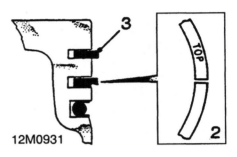

12M0931

2. Fit 2nd compression ring marked 'TOP' with marking uppermost into second groove.
3. Fit 1st compression ring into first groove either way round.

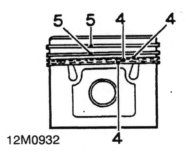

12M0932

4. Position oil control expander ring joint and ring rail gaps all at one side, between gudgeon pin and away from left hand (thrust) side of piston - viewed from front of piston. Space gaps in ring rails approximately 25 mm (1.0 in) each side of expander ring joint.
5. Position compression rings with ring gaps on opposite sides of piston between gudgeon pin and right hand side of piston - viewed from front of piston.
6. Thoroughly clean cylinder bores.
7. Lubricate piston rings and gudgeon pin with engine oil.
8. Lubricate cylinder bores with engine oil.

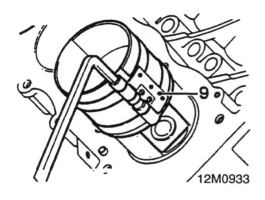

12M0933

9. Fit ring clamp to piston and compress piston rings.

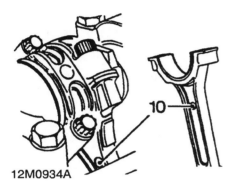

12M0934A

⚠ NOTE: Connecting rods shown in final fitted positions.

10. Insert connecting rod and piston assembly into respective cylinder bore ensuring domed shaped boss on connecting rod faces towards front of engine on RH bank of cylinders, and towards rear on LH bank of cylinders.
11. Fit big-end bearing caps and bearing shells.
12. Fit cylinder head(s).

FLYWHEEL AND STARTER RING GEAR

Flywheel - remove

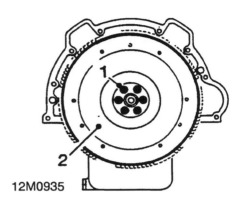

12M0935

1. Restrain crankshaft and remove 6 bolts securing flywheel.
2. Remove flywheel.

⚠ NOTE: Dowel located

Flywheel and starter ring gear - inspection

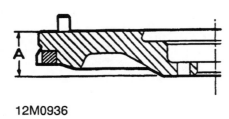

12M0936

1. Inspect flywheel face for cracks, scores and overheating. The flywheel can be refaced on the clutch face providing thickness does not go below minimum.
Flywheel minimum thickness **A** = 40.45 mm (1.6 in)
2. Inspect starter ring gear for worn, chipped and broken teeth.

 CAUTION: Do not attempt to remove reluctor ring.

3. Renew starter ring gear if necessary.

Starter ring gear - renew

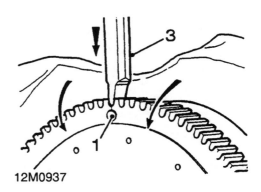

12M0937

1. Drill a 6 mm (0.250 in) diameter hole at root of 2 teeth.

 CAUTION: Do not allow drill to enter flywheel.

2. Secure flywheel in soft jawed vice.
3. Split ring gear using a cold chisel.

 WARNING: Wear safety goggles and take precautions against flying fragments when splitting ring gear.

4. Remove flywheel from vice, remove old ring gear, and place flywheel, clutch side down, on a flat surface.

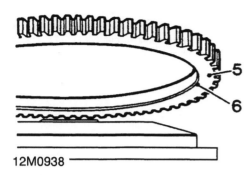

12M0938

1. Fit flywheel and locate on 2 dowels.
2. Fit flywheel bolts.
3. Using assistance, restrain crankshaft and tighten flywheel bolts to 80 Nm (59 lbf.ft).

5. Heat new ring gear uniformly to between 170° and 175° C (340° and 350° F).

 CAUTION: Do not exceed this temperature.

 WARNING: Take care when handling hot ring gear.

6. Locate ring gear on flywheel with chamfered inner diameter towards flywheel flange.

 NOTE: If ring gear is chamfered on both sides, it can be fitted either way round.

7. Press ring gear on to flywheel until it butts against flywheel flange.
8. Allow flywheel to air cool.

DRIVE PLATE AND RING GEAR ASSEMBLY

Drive plate and ring gear assembly - remove - Up to engine nos. 42D00593A and 46D00450A

1. Suitably identify each component to its fitted position.

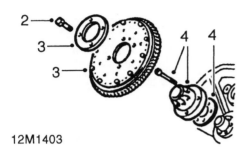

12M1403

△ NOTE: 4.0 litre drive plate illustrated.

2. Remove 4 bolts securing drive plate assembly.
3. Remove buttress ring and drive plate assembly.

△ NOTE: Drive plate assembly is dowel located.

4. Remove 6 socket head cap screws securing hub aligner to crankshaft, remove hub aligner and selective shim; retain shim.

△ NOTE: Dowel located.

Drive plate and ring gear assembly - remove - From engine nos. 42D00594A, 46D00451A and all engines having serial no. prefixes 47D to 51D

1. Suitably identify each component to its fitted position.

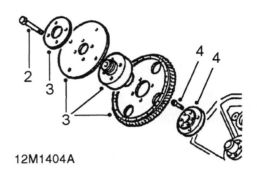

12M1404A

△ NOTE: 4.0 litre drive plate illustrated.

2. Remove 4 bolts securing buttress ring, drive plate, spacer and ring gear assembly to hub aligner.
3. Remove buttress ring, drive plate, spacer and ring gear assembly.

△ NOTE: Ring gear assembly is dowel located.

4. Remove 6 socket head cap screws securing hub aligner to crankshaft, remove hub aligner.

△ NOTE: Dowel located.

Drive plate and ring gear - inspection

1. Inspect drive plate for cracks and distortion.
2. Renew drive plate if necessary.
3. Inspect ring gear for worn, chipped and broken teeth.
4. Renew ring gear assembly if necessary.

Drive plate and ring gear assembly - refit - Up to engine nos. 42D00593A and 46D00450A

⚠ **CAUTION: To prevent distortion to drive plate when bolted to torque converter, drive plate setting height must be checked as follows:**

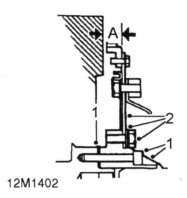

12M1402

1. Fit original selective shim and hub aligner, fit socket head cap screws and tighten to 85 Nm (63 lbf.ft).
2. Fit drive plate assembly and buttress ring ensuring that reference marks are aligned; fit bolts and tighten to 45 Nm (33 lbf.ft).

⚠ **CAUTION: If a new drive plate assembly is being fitted, paint mark on plate must face towards torque converter.**

3. Check the setting height **A**.
   Up to engine no. 42D00593A = 21.25 to 21.37 mm (0.83 to 0.84 in)
   Up to engine no. 46D00450A = 7.69 to 7.81 mm (0.30 to 0.31 in)
4. If setting height is not as specified, remove buttress ring, drive plate assembly, hub aligner and selective shim.

5. Measure existing shim and, if necessary, select appropriate shim to achieve setting height.
   Shims available:
   1.20 - 1.25mm (0.048 to 0.050 in)
   1.30 - 1.35mm (0.051 to 0.053 in)
   1.40 - 1.45mm (0.055 to 0.057 in)
   1.50 - 1.55mm (0.059 to 0.061 in)
   1.60 - 1.65mm (0.063 to 0.065 in)
   1.70 - 1.75mm (0.067 to 0.070 in)
   1.80 - 1.85mm (0.071 to 0.073 in)
   1.90 - 1.95mm (0.075 to 0.077 in)
   2.00 - 2.05mm (0.079 to 0.081 in)
   2.10 - 2.15mm (0.083 to 0.085 in)

6. Fit shim selected, fit hub aligner; fit socket head cap screws and tighten to 85 Nm (63 lbf.ft).
7. Fit drive plate assembly and buttress ring ensuring that reference marks are aligned or that paint mark on replacement drive plate is facing towards torque converter.
8. Fit bolts and tighten to 45 Nm (33 lbf.ft).

Drive plate and ring gear assembly - refit - From engine nos. 42D00594A, 46D00451A and all engines having serial no. prefixes 47D to 51D

 NOTE: It is not necessary to check setting height on drive plates fitted to engines from the above numbers.

1. Fit hub aligner, fit socket head cap screws and tighten to 85 Nm (63 lbf.ft).
2. Fit ring gear assembly, spacer, drive plate and buttress ring ensuring that reference marks are aligned.

⚠ CAUTION: If a new drive plate is being fitted, paint mark must face towards torque converter, ensure holes in plate are aligned with clearance holes in ring gear.

3. Fit bolts and tighten to 45 Nm (33 lbf.ft).

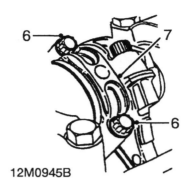

CRANKSHAFT, MAIN AND BIG-END BEARINGS

Big-end bearings - remove

1. Remove sump.

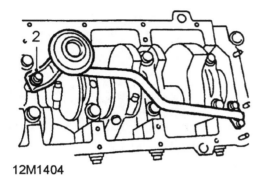

12M1404

2. Remove nut and washers securing oil pick-up pipe to stud.

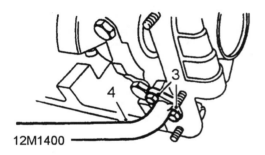

12M1400

3. Remove 2 bolts securing oil pick-up pipe to oil pump cover, withdraw pipe from cover; remove and discard 'O' ring.
4. Remove oil pick-up pipe, recover spacer from stud.
5. Suitably identify bearing caps to their respective connecting rods.

12M0945B

6. Remove 2 bolts securing each bearing cap.
7. Remove bearing cap and bearing shell.

 NOTE: Keep bearing caps and bolts in their fitted order.

8. Push each piston up its respective bore and remove shells from connecting rods.

 NOTE: Big-end bearing shells must be replaced whenever they are removed.

Big-end bearings - refit

1. Fit bearing shells to each connecting rod.

 NOTE: Big-end bearings are available in 0.254 mm (0.01 in) and 0.508 mm (0.02 in) oversizes.

2. Lubricate bearing shells and crankshaft journals with engine oil.
3. Pull connecting rods on to crankshaft journals.
4. Fit bearing shells to each big-end bearing cap.

 NOTE: If crankshaft has been reground, ensure appropriate oversize bearing shells are fitted.

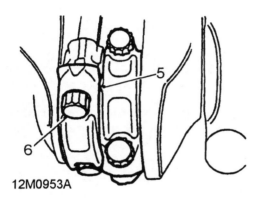

12M0953A

5. Lubricate bearing shells and fit bearing caps ensuring reference marks on connecting rods and bearing caps are aligned.

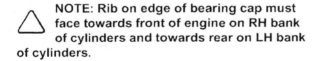 NOTE: Rib on edge of bearing cap must face towards front of engine on RH bank of cylinders and towards rear on LH bank of cylinders.

6. Fit bearing cap bolts and tighten to 20 Nm (15 lbf.ft) then a further 80 degrees.
7. Check connecting rods move freely sideways on crankshaft. Tightness indicates insufficient bearing clearance or misaligned connecting rod.

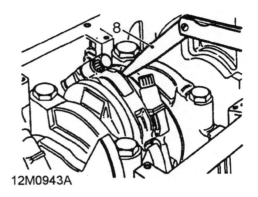

12M0943A

8. Check clearance between connecting rods on each crankshaft journal.
   Connecting rod clearance = 0.15 to 0.36 mm (0.006 to 0.014 in).
9. Clean oil strainer and oil pick-up pipe.
10. Smear a new 'O' ring with engine oil and fit to oil pick-up pipe.
11. Position oil pick-up pipe spacer on number 4 main bearing cap stud.
12. Fit oil pick-up pipe ensuring that end of pipe is correctly inserted in oil pump body.
13. Fit oil pick-up pipe to oil pump body bolts and tighten to 8 Nm (6 lbf.ft).
14. Fit washers and nut securing oil pick-up pipe to stud; tighten nut to 24 Nm (18 lbf.ft).
15. Fit sump.

Crankshaft - remove

1. Remove flywheel or drive plate and ring gear assembly.
2. Remove timing cover.
3. Remove timing gears.
4. Remove big-end bearings.

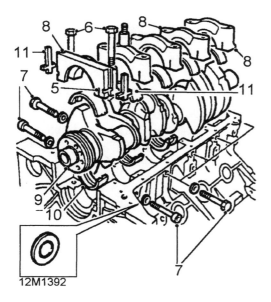

12M1392

5. Make suitable reference marks between each main bearing cap and cylinder block.
6. Starting at centre main bearing and working outwards, progressively slacken then remove 10 main bearing cap bolts.

 CAUTION: Keep bolts in their fitted order.

7. Starting at centre main bearing and working outwards, progressively slacken then remove 5 LH side hexagonal head bolts and 4 RH side hexagonal head bolts and one socket head cap bolt; remove and discard Dowty washers.
8. Remove 5 main bearing caps, remove and discard bearing shells.

 NOTE: Number 4 main bearing cap is drilled to accommodate oil pick-up pipe stud.

9. Lift out crankshaft; remove and discard rear oil seal.
10. Remove and discard 5 bearing shells from cylinder block.

 CAUTION: Main bearing shells must be replaced whenever they are removed.

11. Remove and discard side seals from rear main bearing cap.
12. Remove all traces of sealant from bearing cap and cylinder block.
13. Remove Woodruff key from crankshaft.

Knock sensor - remove

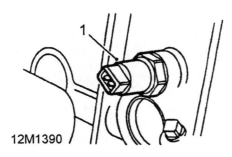

12M1390

1. Remove knock sensor from cylinder block.

Crankshaft position sensor - remove

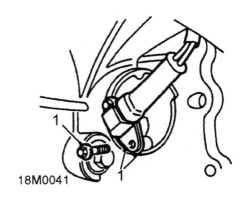

18M0041

1. Remove 2 bolts securing crankshaft position sensor to gearbox adaptor plate, remove sensor; collect spacer - if fitted.

Crankshaft - inspection

1. Clean crankshaft and blow out oil passages.

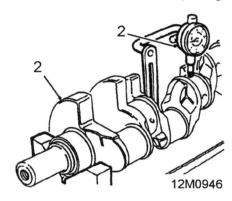

12M0946

2. Support crankshaft front and rear bearing journals on vee blocks, and using a DTI, measure run-out on centre main bearing. Maximum permitted run-out = 0.08 mm (0.003 in).
   If run-out exceeds permitted maximum, crankshaft is unsuitable for regrinding and should be replaced.

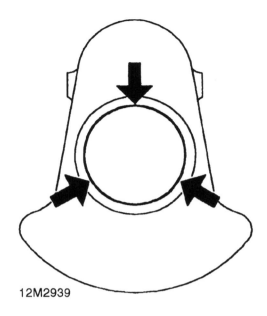

12M2939

3. Measure each journal for overall wear and ovality, take 3 measurements at 120° intervals at each end and centre of journals.
   Main bearing journal diameter = 63.487 to 63.500 mm (2.499 to 2.52 in)
   Maximum out of round = 0.040 mm (0.002 in).
   Big-end bearing journal diameter = 55.500 to 55.513 mm (2.20 to 2.22 in)
   Maximum out of round = 0.040 mm (0.002 in).
   If measurements exceed permitted maximum, regrind or fit new crankshaft.

⚠ NOTE: Ovality checks should be made at 120° intervals around each journal.
Crankshaft main and big-end bearings are available in 0.254 mm (0.01 in) and 0.508 mm (0.02 in) oversizes.

Crankshaft dimensions:

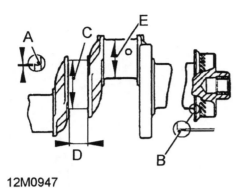

12M0947

Bearing journal radius - all journals except rear main journal **A** = 1.90 to 2.28 mm (0.075 to 0.09 in).
Rear main bearing journal radius **B** = 3.04 mm (0.12 in).

Bearing journal diameter **C**:
Standard = 63.487 to 63.500 mm (2.499 to 2.52 in).
0.254 mm (0.01 in) undersize = 63.233 to 63.246 mm (2.511 to 2.512 in).
0.508 mm (0.02 in) undersize = 62.979 to 62.992 mm (2.509 to 2.510 in).

Bearing journal width **D**:
Standard = 26.975 to 27.026 mm (1.061 to 1.064 in).

Bearing journal diameter **E**:
Standard = 55.500 to 55.513 mm (2.20 to 2.22 in).
0.254 mm (0.01 in) undersize = 55.246 to 55.259 mm (2.17 to 2.18 in).
0.508 mm (0.02 in) undersize = 54.992 to 55.005 mm (2.16 to 2.165 in).

⚠ **CAUTION: if crankshaft is to be replaced, ensure replacement is correct for engine being overhauled. Crankshafts are not interchangeable between 4.0 and 4.6 litre engines.**

1. Check crankshaft spigot bearing for wear, renew if necessary.

Crankshaft spigot bearing - renew

1. Carefully extract old spigot bearing.
2. Clean bearing recess in crankshaft.

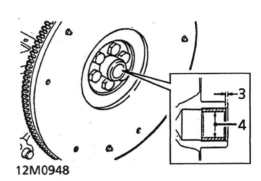

12M0948

3. Fit new bearing flush with, or to a maximum of 1.6 mm (0.06 in) below end face of crankshaft.
4. Ream bearing to correct inside diameter. Spigot bearing inside diameter = 19.177 + 0.025 - 0.000 mm (0.75 + 0.001 - 0.000 in).
5. Remove all traces of swarf.

Crankshaft - refit

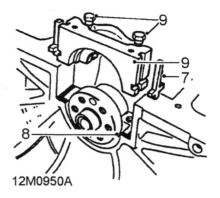

12M0950A

1. Clean main bearing caps, bearing shell recesses and mating surfaces of cylinder block.

 CAUTION: Ensure bolt holes in cylinder block and main bearing caps are clean and dry.

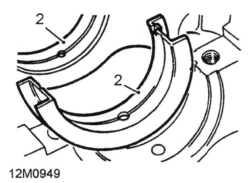

12M0949

2. Fit new upper main bearing shells, with oil holes and grooves, in cylinder block, ensuring flanged shell is fitted in centre position.

 NOTE: If crankshaft has been reground ensure appropriate oversize bearing shells are fitted.

3. Lubricate main bearing shells with engine oil and position crankshaft in cylinder block.
4. Fit new main bearing shells to bearing caps.
5. Lubricate main bearing shells with engine oil.
6. Fit numbers 1 to 4 main bearing caps ensuring that reference marks made during dismantling are aligned, fit and tighten main bearing cap bolts to 5 Nm (4 lbf.ft).

NOTE: Do not fit side bolts at this stage.

7. Fit side seals to rear main bearing cap.

 CAUTION: Seals must protrude approximately 1.5 mm (0.05 in) above bearing cap face.

8. Apply a 3 mm (0.12 in) wide bead of Hylomar PL32 jointing compound to bearing cap rear mating face on cylinder block.

CAUTION: Ensure sealant does not enter bolt holes.

9. Lubricate rear main bearing shell and side seals with engine oil, carefully fit rear main bearing cap assembly; fit and tighten main bearing cap bolts to 5 Nm (4 lbf.ft).

 CAUTION: Ensure that engine oil does not enter side bolt holes in bearing cap.

10. Smear new Dowty washers with engine oil and fit to main bearing cap side bolts.
11. Fit and tighten RH then LH side bolts to 5 Nm (4 lbf.ft) ensuring that socket head cap bolt is fitted to rear main bearing cap on RH side of cylinder block adjacent to starter motor aperture.

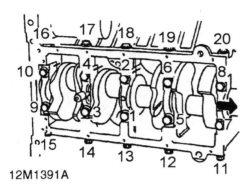

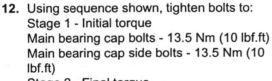

12M1391A

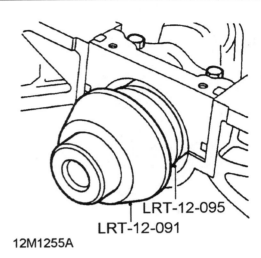

LRT-12-095
LRT-12-091

12M1255A

12. Using sequence shown, tighten bolts to:
Stage 1 - Initial torque
Main bearing cap bolts - 13.5 Nm (10 lbf.ft)
Main bearing cap side bolts - 13.5 Nm (10 lbf.ft)
Stage 2 - Final torque
Main bearing cap bolts numbers 1 to 8 - 72 Nm (53 lbf.ft)
Main bearing cap bolts numbers 9 and 10 - 92 Nm (68 lbf.ft)
Main bearing cap side bolts 11 to 20 - 45 Nm (33 lbf.ft)
13. Trim off excess material from rear main bearing cap side seals.
14. Clean seal location and running surface on crankshaft.
15. Clean seal protector **LRT-12-095** and lubricate with engine oil.
16. Lubricate oil seal lip with engine oil.

17. Position seal protector **LRT-12-095** to crankshaft.
18. Fit seal using tool **LRT-12-091**.
19. Fit Woodruff key to crankshaft.
20. Check crankshaft end-float.

⚠ NOTE: If 0.508 mm (0.02 in) oversize main bearings have been fitted, it may be necessary to machine thrust faces of crankshaft centre main bearing location to achieve correct end-float. Ensure an equal amount of material is removed from each thrust face.

21. Fit big-end bearings.
22. Fit timing cover and gears.
23. Fit flywheel or drive plate and ring gear assembly.
24. Fit sump.

Crankshaft end - float - check

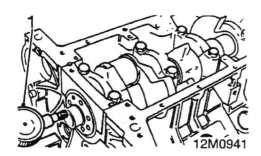

12M0941

1. Set-up DTI to measure end float.
2. Move crankshaft forwards and zero gauge.
3. Move crankshaft rearwards, record end-float reading obtained.
   Crankshaft end-float = 0.10 to 0.20 mm (0.004 to 0.008 in).
4. Remove DTI.

⚠ NOTE: Crankshaft end-float is controlled by thrust faces on upper half of centre main bearing shell. If crankshaft has been reground and 0.508 mm (0.02 in) oversize main bearing shells are to be fitted, it may be necessary to machine thrust faces of crankshaft centre main bearing journal to achieve correct end-float. Ensure an equal amount of material is removed from each thrust face.

Knock sensor - refit

1. Clean threads of knock sensor and mating threads in cylinder block.
2. Fit knock sensor and tighten to 16 Nm (12 lbf.ft).

⚠ CAUTION: Do not apply any type of sealant to threads.

Crankshaft position sensor - refit

1. Position crankshaft position sensor and spacer - if fitted to gearbox adaptor plate, fit bolts and tighten to 6 Nm (4 lbf.ft).

Brooklands Books Ltd., PO Box 146, Cobham, Surrey KT11 1LG, England Phone: (44) 1932 865051
E-mail: sales@brooklands-books.com www.brooklandsbooks.com

ISBN: 9781855205284   Part No. LRL 0166ENG   Ref: LRP3WH   1T4/2033

LAND ROVER OFFICIAL FACTORY PUBLICATIONS

Land Rover Series 1 Workshop Manual	4291
Land Rover Series 1 1948-53 Parts Catalogue	4051
Land Rover Series 1 1954-58 Parts Catalogue	4107
Land Rover Series 1 Instruction Manual	4277
Land Rover Series 1 and II Diesel Instruction Manual	4343
Land Rover Series II and IIA Workshop Manual	AKM8159
Land Rover Series II and Early IIA Bonneted Control Parts Catalogue	605957
Land Rover Series IIA Bonneted Control Parts Catalogue	RTC9840CC
Land Rover Series IIA, III and 109 V8 Optional Equipment Parts Catalogue	RTC9842CE
Land Rover Series IIA/IIB Instruction Manual	LSM64IM
Land Rover Series 2A and 3 88 Parts Catalogue Supplement (USA Spec)	606494
Land Rover Series III Workshop Manual	AKM3648
Land Rover Series III Workshop Manual V8 Supplement (edn. 2)	AKM8022
Land Rover Series III 88, 109 and 109 V8 Parts Catalogue	RTC9841CE
Land Rover Series III Owners Manual 1971-1978	607324B
Land Rover Series III Owners Manual 1979-1985	AKM8155
Military Land Rover (Lightweight) Series III Parts Catalogue	61278
Military Land Rover Series III (L.W.B.) User Handbook	608179
Military Land Rover (Lightweight) Series III User Manual	608180
Land Rover 90/110 and Defender Workshop Manual 1983-1992	SLR621ENWM
Land Rover Defender Workshop Manual 1993-1995	LDAWMEN93
Land Rover Defender 300 Tdi and Supplements Workshop Manual 1996-1998	LRL0097ENGBB
Land Rover Defender Td5 Workshop Manual and Supplements 1999-2006	LRL0410BB
Land Rover Defender Electrical Manual Td5 1999-06 and 300Tdi 2002-2006	LRD5EHBB
Land Rover 110 Parts Catalogue 1983-1986	RTC9863CE
Land Rover Defender Parts Catalogue 1987-2006	STC9021CC
Land Rover 90 • 110 Handbook 1983-1990 MY	LSM0054
Land Rover Defender 90 • 110 • 130 Handbook 1991 MY - Feb. 1994	LHAHBEN93
Land Rover Defender 90 • 110 • 130 Handbook Mar. 1994 - 1998 MY	LRL0087ENG/2
Military Land Rover 90/110 All Variants (Excluding APV and SAS) User Manual	2320-D-122-201
Military Land Rover 90 and 110 2.5 Diesel Engine Versions User Handbook	SLR989WDHB
Military Land Rover Defender XD - Wolf Workshop Manual - 2320D128 -	302 522 523 524
Military Land Rover Defender XD - Wolf Parts Catalogue	2320D128711
Discovery Workshop Manual 1990-1994 (petrol 3.5, 3.9, Mpi and diesel 200 Tdi)	SJR900ENWM
Discovery Workshop Manual 1995-1998 (petrol 2.0 Mpi, 3.9, 4.0 V8 and diesel 300 Tdi)	LRL0079BB
Discovery Series II Workshop Manual 1999-2003 (petrol 4.0 V8 and diesel Td5 2.5)	VDR100090/6
Discovery Parts Catalogue 1989-1998 (2.0 Mpi, 3.5, 3.9 V8 and 200 Tdi and 300 Tdi)	RTC9947CF
Discovery Parts Catalogue 1999-2003 (petrol 4.0 V8 and diesel Td5 2.5)	STC9049CA
Discovery Owners Handbook 1990-1991 (petrol 3.5 V8 and diesel 200 Tdi)	SJR820ENHB90
Discovery Series II Handbook 1999-2004 MY (petrol 4.0 V8 and Td5 diesel)	LRL0459BB
Freelander Workshop Manual 1998-2000 (petrol 1.8 and diesel 2.0)	LRL0144
Freelander Workshop Manual 2001-2003 ON (petrol 1.8L, 2.5L and diesel Td4 2.0)	LRL0350ENG/4
Land Rover 101 1 Tonne Forward Control Workshop Manual	RTC9120
Land Rover 101 1 Tonne Forward Control Parts Catalogue	608294B
Land Rover 101 1 Tonne Forward Control User Manual	608239
Range Rover Workshop Manual 1970-1985 (petrol 3.5)	AKM3630
Range Rover Workshop Manual 1986-1989	SRR660ENWM &
(petrol 3.5 and diesel 2.4 Turbo VM)	LSM180WS4/2
Range Rover Workshop Manual 1990-1994	
(petrol 3.9, 4.2 and diesel 2.5 Turbo VM, 200 Tdi)	LHAWMENA02
Range Rover Workshop Manual 1995-2001 (petrol 4.0, 4.6 and BMW 2.5 diesel)	LRL0326ENGBB
Range Rover Workshop Manual 2002-2005 (BMW petrol 4.4 and BMW 3.0 diesel)	LRL0477
Range Rover Electrical Manual 2002-2005 UK version (petrol 4.4 and 3.0 diesel)	RR02KEMBB
Range Rover Electrical Manual 2002-2005 USA version (BMW petrol 4.4)	RR02AEMBB
Range Rover Parts Catalogue 1970-1985 (petrol 3.5)	RTC9846CH
Range Rover Parts Catalogue 1986-1991 (petrol 3.5, 3.9 and diesel 2.4 and 2.5 Turbo VM)	RTC9908CB
Range Rover Parts Catalogue 1992-1994 MY and 95 MY Classic	
(petrol 3.9, 4.2 and diesel 2.5 Turbo VM, 200 Tdi and 300 Tdi)	RTC9961CB
Range Rover Parts Catalogue 1995-2001 MY (petrol 4.0, 4.6 and BMW 2.5 diesel)	RTC9970CE
Range Rover Owners Handbook 1970-1980 (petrol 3.5)	606917
Range Rover Owners Handbook 1981-1982 (petrol 3.5)	AKM8139
Range Rover Owners Handbook 1983-1985 (petrol 3.5)	LSM0001HB
Range Rover Owners Handbook 1986-1987 (petrol 3.5 and diesel 2.4 Turbo VM)	LSM129HB

Engine Overhaul Manuals for Land Rover and Range Rover

300 Tdi Engine, R380 Manual Gearbox and LT230T Transfer Gearbox Overhaul Manuals	LRL003, 070 & 081
Petrol Engine V8 3.5, 3.9, 4.0, 4.2 and 4.6 Overhaul Manuals	LRL004 & 164
Land Rover/Range Rover Driving Techniques	LR369
Working in the Wild - Manual for Africa	SMR684MI
Winching in Safety - Complete guide to winching Land Rovers and Range Rovers	SMR699MI

Workshop Manual Owners Edition

Land Rover 2 / 2A / 3 Owners Workshop Manual 1959-1983
Land Rover 90, 110 and Defender Workshop Manual Owners Edition 1983-1995
Land Rover Discovery Workshop Manual Owners Edition 1990-1998

All titles available from Amazon or Land Rover specialists
Brooklands Books Ltd., P.O. Box 146, Cobham, Surrey, KT11 1LG, England, UK
Phone: +44 (0) 1932 865051   info@brooklands-books.com   www.brooklands-books.com

www.brooklandsbooks.com

Printed in Great Britain
by Amazon

58464112R00075